c ds

Tim Rock

MELBOURNE | LONDON | OAKLAND

Cayman Islands

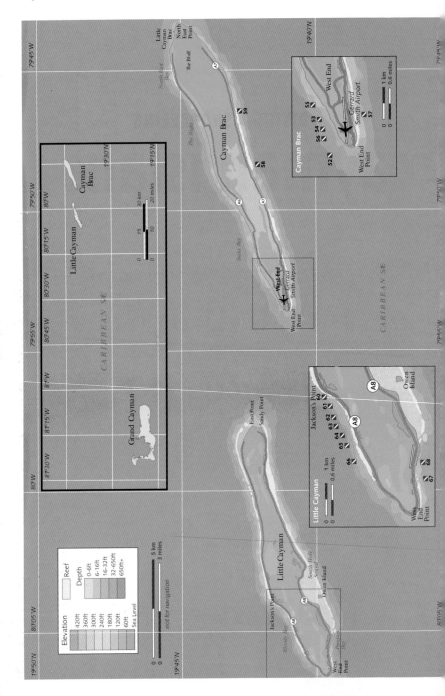

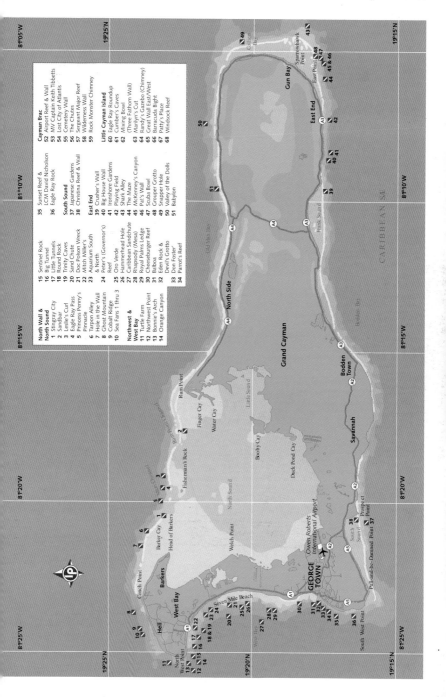

Cayman Islands

North Wall & North Sound
1 Stingray City
2 Sandbar
3 Leslie's Curl
4 Eagle Ray Pass
5 Princess Penny's Pinnacle
6 Tarpon Alley
7 Hole in the Wall
8 Ghost Mountain
9 Cobalt Ridge
10 Sea Fans 1 thru 3

Northwest & West Bay
11 Turtle Farm
12 Northwest Point
13 Bonnie's Arch
14 Orange Canyon

15 Sentinel Rock
16 Big Tunnel
17 Little Tunnels
18 Round Rock
19 Trinity Caves
20 Sand Chute
21 Doc Poison Wreck
22 Mitch Miller's
23 Aquarium South & North
24 Peter's (Governor's) Reef
25 Oro Verde
26 Hammerhead Hole
27 Caribbean Sandchute
28 Rhapsody (Mesa)
29 Royal Palms Ledge
30 Cheeseburger Reef
31 Balboa
32 Eden Rock & Devil's Grotto
33 Don Foster
34 Parrot's Reef

35 Sunset Reef & LCM David Nicholson
36 Eagle Ray Rock

South Sound
37 Japanese Gardens
38 Christina Reef & Wall

East End
39 Crusher's Wall
40 Big House Wall
41 Ironshore Gardens
42 Playing Field
43 Shark Alley
44 The Maze
45 McKenney's Canyon
46 Pat's Wall
47 Scuba Bowl
48 Grouper Grotto
49 Snapper Hole
50 Valley of the Dolls
51 Babylon

Cayman Brac
52 Airport Reef & Wall
53 MV Captain Keith Tibbetts
54 Lost City of Atlantis
55 Cemetery Wall
56 The Chutes
57 Sergeant Major Reef
58 Wilderness Wall
59 Rock Monster Chimney

Little Cayman Island
60 Eagle Ray Roundup
61 Cumber's Caves
62 Mixing Bowl (Three Fathom Wall)
63 Marilyn's Cut
64 Randy's Gazebo (Chimney)
65 Great Wall East/West
66 Barracuda Bight
67 Patty's Place
68 Windsock Reef

Diving & Snorkeling Cayman Islands
2nd edition – August 2007

Published by
Lonely Planet Publications Pty Ltd
ABN 36 005 607 983
90 Maribyrnong St, Footscray,
Victoria, 3011, Australia
www.lonelyplanet.com

Lonely Planet Offices
Australia Locked Bag 1, Footscray, Victoria, 3011
Phone 03 8379 8000 Fax 03 8379 8111
Email talk2us@lonelyplanet.com.au

USA 150 Linden St, Oakland, CA 94607
Phone 510 893 8555 Toll free 800 275 8555 Fax 510 893 8572
Email info@lonelyplanet.com

UK 72-82 Rosebery Ave London EC1R 4RW
Phone 020 7841 9000 Fax 020 7841 9001
Email go@lonelyplanet.co.uk

Author Tim Rock
Publisher Roz Hopkins
Associate Publisher Chris Rennie
Commissioning Editors Ben Handicott & Bridget Blair
Design Manager Brendan Dempsey
Mapping Development Paul Piaia
Cartography Anita Banh, Wayne Murphy
Production Pepper Publishing (Aust) Pty Ltd
Print Production Manager Graham Imeson

Printed by Hang Tai Printing Company
Printed in China
Photographs Tim Rock (unless otherwise noted)

ISBN 978 1 74059 897 2

With Many Thanks to
Mark Griffiths, Yvonne Kirk, Angus Fleetwood,
Tom Calderwood, Sayher Heffernan

Contents

Author

TIM ROCK

Tim Rock attended the journalism program at the University of Nebraska–Omaha and has been a professional broadcast and print photojournalist for over 30 years. The majority of those years has been spent in the Western and Indo Pacific region reporting on environmental and conservation issues.

His television series, *Aquaquest Micronesia,* was an Ace Award finalist. He has also produced six documentaries on the history and undersea fauna of the region. Tim won the prestigious Excellence in the Use of Photography award from the Society of Publishers in Asia, amongst many other awards for photography and writing. He publishes a magazine and works as a correspondent for numerous Pacific Rim magazines. Tim is the author of many Diving & Snorkeling series guides including *Bonaire, Belize, Thailand, Chuuk Lagoon-Pohnpei-Kosrae, Bali & Lombok, Guam & Yap, Palau, South Africa-Mozambique* and *Papua New Guinea,* and is a major contributor to *Philippines*.

FROM THE AUTHOR

A warm thank you to my wife, Larie, for her support and help in my travels and the writing of this guide. I would also like to thank Olga Spoelstra for her many talents and unselfish help and friendship in making images and words

for this book. Special thanks to Jonathan Dietz, Nancy Easterbrook, Leslie Agnostelli, Courtney Platt, Anne Louise Tuke, Jerry Beatty, Joanne Gammage, Mike Sutton-Brown, Carol Zawistowski, Jerome Begot, Nancy Leone Easterbrook, Jay Warner Easterbrook, Brandee Milman, Gregory Beyette, Eleanore Head, Zelda Norden, Nathanial Robb II, Joshua Williamson, Susan Dasher, Gary Nightingale, Javan Roberts, James Strawson, Steve Tippetts, Lee Garwood, Mark Leibbrandt, Anton Swanepoel, Melissa Rivers, Arie Barendrecht, Dora Valdez, Ian Kingsley, Britta Egrid, Spencer Mason, Sean Crothers, Leanne Strik and Cathy Church, who all shared some great insights about their beloved Cayman Island waters. And thank you to the people of Cayman Islands for their hospitality and dedication to the preservation of the marine world that surrounds their beautiful island.

FROM THE PUBLISHER

The Cayman Islands are one of diving's best-known destinations. Grand Cayman has made marine interaction famous with its **Stingray City**, and ushered many people into the amazing world of SCUBA due to its clear, warm waters and many training facilities. We are happy to present this new guide for the snorkel and dive sites of the three Cayman Islands and hope you enjoy the beautiful marine walls, reefs and creatures.

PHOTO NOTES

Tim uses Nikon digital cameras, Aquatica underwater housings and Ikelite strobes. Tim's photographic work is represented by Lonely Planet Images (www.lonelyplanetimages.com), Double Blue Images (www.doubleblue.com) and other agents worldwide.

Introduction

The Cayman Islands are synonymous with scuba diving. Lauded as the birthplace of sport diving in the Caribbean, the rather small and low Grand Cayman is big on marine features. It is blessed with deep drop-offs, the proverbial 'gin' clear water, and the protected bays that make a scuba experience somewhere on its coast a daily fact of life. If you want to get beneath the sea, there is always somewhere here to explore.

Endowed with a tax-free status, there is a bit of banking center bustle on the main island. This combined with a hotel row along a stunning beach makes Grand Cayman an active place to visit day and night.

The nearby isles of Little Cayman and Cayman Brac, often referred to as The Sisters, are equally blessed with underwater treasures. They are also geared for diving and visitors will find a much more laid back atmosphere of sunsets and coconut palms than on the main island.

Hammered by a major hurricane (Ivan) in 2004, the Cayman Islands have bounced back with renewed vigor and Grand Cayman is seizing the moment to expand roads, hotel space and condominium development while courting an ever-increasing number of cruise liners and airlines. These deposit day trippers, and week- and month-long visitors to the main island and The Sisters.

At just a little over an hour's hop from Miami, the islands sit on a shelf of deep, blue water just south of Cuba. The water clarity and close proximity to the United States, combined with consistent warm ocean temperatures, make this an ideal destination for those wanting to get their gills wet. It is considered a must for everyone's log book.

This guide introduces various sites that can be dived both from the beach and by boat from the main island of Grand Cayman. It is known for its clear waters, sponge encrusted canyons and fish covered pinnacles highlight some the island's deeper dives. Shallow dives feature shipwrecks, caves with lurking tarpon and fascinating invertebrate life. At **Stingray City,** one of diving's most famous novelty sites, divers interact with amazingly friendly reef rays that arrive in big numbers at the sound of a boat.

Also featured are the sites of The Sister islands and their famous sheer drop-offs that are a magnet for all kinds of marine life. Nature-lovers will feel right at home while viewing Cayman Brac's rugged limestone cliffs and flocks of parrots and Little Cayman's amazing bird sanctuary and lazy iguanas. It's not hard to see

Red rope sponges extend from a Cayman reef

why snorkelers love these islands and divers rave about the sheer drop-offs, shipwrecks and even a 'lost city'.

The Cayman Islands have so many sites that they are too numerous for a single volume. We have attempted to select some of the most popular and action-packed dives the islands have to offer for this guide, in order to give divers and snorkelers a good feel for the broad offerings that the islands hold in store.

CAYMAN ISLANDS DIVE HIGHLIGHTS

1 **Stingray City** – a favorite of snorkelers and divers who interact with dozens of amazingly gentle stingrays in only 12 feet of water.
2 **Ghost Mountain** – great undersea pinnacle on the North Sound, full of big groupers and other marine life.
3 **Bonnie's Arch** – beautiful natural arch with delicate corals, many juvenile fish and roaming lobsters.
4 **Doc Polson Wreck** – a shallow ship with very good macro life that's fun and easy to explore.
5 **Babylon** – one of the signature wall dives of Grand Cayman – beautiful sponges, fans, black coral and big fish can be found here.
6 **Turtle Reef** – a snorkel and dive site which has a great tarpon cave and-can be visited by boat or walk-in.
7 **Orange Canyon** – large elephant ear sponges give the reef bright color and lots of fish and turtles come here.
8 **Bloody Bay (Great Wall)** – explore the most famous drop-off wall, with its rich sponge and coral life.
9 **MV Captain Keith Tibbetts** – a must dive, this former Russian frigate is intact with guns ready for photographers.
10 **Randy's Gazebo** – the formations and fish life make this an interesting immersion.

Heading out through the aqua waters of the North Sound

Facts about the Cayman Islands

OVERVIEW

The Cayman Islands aren't big, but Grand Cayman and the two 'sister' islands of Little Cayman and Cayman Brac are big time destinations on most divers' lists. The clear waters, wide range of hotels and training options, numerous and varied dive sites and established infrastructure combine with its close proximity to the USA to make it one of the most popular dive destinations in the world. The islands even claim to be the 'birth place of diving in the Caribbean'.

Grand Cayman, Cayman Brac and Little Cayman are also distinctly different and offer varying diving attractions as well as unique topside experiences. Grand Cayman's **Stingray City** is billed as 'the world's best 12-foot dive,' Little Cayman's 'Bloody Bay Wall' is legendary for its near-vertical drop-off, and Cayman Brac has the northern hemisphere's only diveable Russian wreck. This guide describes 68 of the Cayman's best dive sites.

Oddly, you may not see many Caymanians if you're in the Cayman's on a diving holiday. That's because many of them are bankers (with briefcases and cell phones), real estate brokers, or involved in the burgeoning hotel and condominium industry. Scuba divers are more likely to run into Brits, Americans and Canadians escaping the cold climes to earn their living working in wetsuits under the sun.

Rebuilding after the devastating hurricane in 2004 is at a frenetic pace, but there is still an island vibe despite the ubiquitous construction cranes and daily gaggle of cruise ships. The colorful coral reefs, ravenous stingrays, bright night lights, various eateries and soft reggae beats on the street make Grand Cayman keep Grand Cayman and its 'sisters' at the top of the diving checklist.

Snorkeling at Rum Point

Grand Cayman has been heavily influenced by American culture, especially in George Town and the resorts along Seven Mile Beach. In the smaller villages and on Little Cayman and Cayman Brac, the culture is more traditionally West Indian, although the British influence is close to the surface. English is, after all, the only language spoken on the islands, and the Queen's birthday is celebrated every June with a parade and 21-gun salute. West Indian traditions are noticeable in the *soca*, calypso and reggae you'll hear emanating from locals' jeeps, clubs and bars.

Thanks to a thriving tourism and cruiseship industry, resorts and condos have sprung up everywhere, and you can count on every convenience, from air-con and cold beer to swanky shopping and ESPN. But if you want to get away from it all, it's easy to escape the satellite dishes and slickness. Just slip underwater.

HISTORY

The Cayman Islands' history has an early blank space, but is well-documented after explorers started plying the Caribbean seas. Aboriginal inhabitants have left no trace of their existence. The first human known to have laid eyes on the islands was Christopher Columbus, who in 1503 spotted a swarm of turtles around Cayman Brac and Little Cayman and named the islands Tortugas (Spanish for turtles). The name actually changed a few times, but by the time Francis Drake got to Grand Cayman in 1586, the islands were commonly known as Caymanas, a Carib word for the crocodiles that live on Grand Cayman and were used as a food source for sailors along with the sea turtles.

For the next century or so, the Caymans were used by some pretty famous pirates. There are still legends of buried pirate treasure on the islands and there's a pirate cave to see on Grand Cayman. There were no permanent settlers until the 1660s, when a couple of deserters from the British army came over from Jamaica. In 1670, the islands became a possession of the British Crown, falling under Jamaican administration.

Aside from cotton farming and turtle hunting, the major early occupation was wrecking – salvaging the remains of ships that ran aground. The most famous of these disasters is the Wreck of the Ten Sails, which occurred when a ship struck a reef in 1794, causing a chain reaction involving nine other vessels. According to legend, the Caymanians went to such

Aerial view of George Town

A restored 1800s Cayman house

lengths to aid the shipwrecked that a grateful George III granted the islands a tax-free status. That is still in place today and has made Grand Cayman a world financial center.

After slavery was abolished in 1835, most freed slaves remained on the islands, and by 1900 the Caymans' people dealt in cotton, mahogany, sarsaparilla, thatch rope (mostly exported to Jamaica), fishing, turtle hunting and shipbuilding. Tourism and banking took over during the mid-20th century.

Divers then put the Caymans Islands on the international tourist map and continue to do so.

By the 1960s, tourists went from being seen as pests to being seen as cash cows. They began fashioning the tax structure that's made Grand Cayman a center of offshore banking (there are more financial institutions here than in New York City) and the infrastructure that's made it a capital of Caribbean tourism. The 1960s also saw the islands shrug off Jamaican stewardship and place themselves directly under the British Crown.

This semi-independent country is the fifth-largest financial center in the world. After long being viewed as a potential haven for money-laundering activities, international observers now agree that it has effectively cleaned up its financial sector.

Cleaning up was also first on the agenda after Hurricane Ivan devastated Grand Cayman in September 2004.

DIVING HISTORY

Recreational scuba diving began in the Cayman Islands in 1957, when dive operator Bob Soto brought the concept to Grand Cayman and opened its first dive shop. Up until that time, scuba diving was pretty much only done commercially or for marine research. His move transformed it into playtime for the general public, and is considered to be the birth of Caribbean sport diving. With Mike Nelson and *Sea Hunt* hitting US television and fueling interest in this adventurous sport, interest slowly grew. Soto also invented the concept of the dive package.

Today, the Caymans are one of the world's top dive destinations, with more than 40 dive operations and 200 sites. Locals were reluctant to accept diving, but when they saw that divers and their tourist dollars meant the construction of an airport, hotels and road improvements, they quickly got on board. In the 1970s, tourism really took off. Now, next to banking, it is Cayman's top industry.

The Caymans also came under the wing of the publisher of *Skin Diver Magazine*, Paul Tzimoulis, whose profound influence on the dive industry put the Caymans permanently on the map. Tzimoulis named and constantly promoted Stingray City and helped Wayne Hasson start the live aboard Cayman Aggressor before live aboards were common. He also helped pioneer Ron Kipp build one of the world's largest dive operations on Grand Cayman. Don Foster's Diving was another pioneer operation that continues today in two locations. Captain Crosby Ebanks, in business for 44 years, is credited with being first to feed the stingrays by hand. Cathy Church pioneered dive photography instruction and still teaches today.

In The Sisters, Sam McCoy has also been a true pioneer, starting when there was no electricity on Little Cayman. Today, a new generation of forward-thinking people has taken the reins and the Cayman future looks bright and leads the way in the Caribbean.

GEOGRAPHY

Grand Cayman Island is a small place with a big inner bay and not a lot of elevation. Sparsely populated, mostly flat and partly marshy, Grand Cayman, Cayman Brac and Little Cayman have a corner of the Caribbean all to themselves. The Sister Islands of Cayman Brac and Little Cayman, which lie approximately 89 miles east-northeast of Grand Cayman, are separated from each other by a channel about seven miles wide.

A huge bronze propeller and an old lead keel are attractions at the 1794 wreck of the Ten Sails Park.

7 Mile Beach's famous sunset attracts a dusk jogger

Serving tourists fresh coconuts

The largest island, Grand Cayman, is shaped a bit like the Little Dipper and spans about 25 miles (45km) from the lip of the cup on the western end to the tip of the handle on the eastern end. Little Cayman and Cayman Brac are both about 10 miles long and one mile wide (16km long and 2km wide).

The three islands are limestone outcroppings, the tops of a submarine mountain range called the Cayman Ridge. This extends west-southwest from the Sierra Maestra range off the southeast part of Cuba to the Misteriosa Bank near Belize. The islands lack rivers or streams because of the porous nature of the limestone rock. This lack of runoff is a boon for divers, as it normally gives all of the islands exceptional visibility, often well over 120ft.

Between the Cayman Islands and Jamaica lies the deepest part of the Caribbean, the Cayman Trough, which is over four miles deep. South of Cayman is the Bartlett Deep where depths of over 18,000ft have been recorded.

CLIMATE

The Cayman Islands' tropical but pleasant climate is one of its biggest attractions. The weather is warm all year and winters are quite mild. High 80°Fs (low 30°Cs) are a regular occurrence virtually every day of the year, with temperatures rarely peaking above that. Evenings are also warm and mild. Rain tends to fall in short bursts between May and November, with the chance of hurricanes most likely between August and October. October and November into December can also have spells of wind, but these conditions are usually accompanied by blue skies.

POPULATION, PEOPLE & CULTURE

There are about 44,000 permanent residents on the three Cayman Islands, though Grand Cayman is by far the most populous. As the islands were administered from British-held Jamaica from 1863 until 1962, Cayman islanders are a combination of Caribbean (mostly Jamaican) and European (mainly British) descent but are also greatly influenced by Americans. They enjoy the highest standard of living in the Caribbean and also have fine systems of education, health care and infrastructure.

The Cayman Islands' governor is appointed by the Queen of England. The legislators and ex-official members who are appointed by the governor make the laws of the islands. Politics is an active pastime on the islands.

It is estimated that more than 90 nationalities can be found in this small population base, making it a true melting pot. It is difficult to become a permanent resident and most work permits are granted for only seven years or less. This makes the transient population quite large and many of these people work in the tourist and dive industry. Many resident Caymanians are involved in offshore banking and real estate.

Cayman ladies

George Town's seaside

LANGUAGES

The official language of the Cayman Islands is English, which is spoken most everywhere. There's a Caymanian twist to some English words which makes it a pleasant dialect to hear. Today there are many influences, as there are said to be more than 90 nationalities living and working in the islands. But English is by far the most used language and it will work most everywhere on all three islands.

GATEWAY CITY

The first look many tourists, especially those thousands arriving by cruise ship, get of the Caymans is the bustling little burg of George Town. The face of the town is made up from a strange conglomeration of hip and chain bars like Guy Harvey's, beachside Hammerheads and the Hard Rock Café, traditional and historic wooden buildings that managed to survive the hurricane surge of 2004 and some newly erected waterfront shopping centers. Busy blocks inside the city hold numerous banks and high-end jewelry and watch shops, including black coral galleries which maintain they are harvesting the precious coral in a conservation-minded manner. The

THE CASTLE B...

ST. LOUIS, MO

Leslie   1244 NM →

BUENOS AIRES
3491 NM
CENTINA

MELISSA

PHILLY PA USA

MEL

The international sign at dive
pioneer Don Foster's shoreline

Carved masks at the downtown craft market

artistic pendants and sculptures made from this black coral are truly stunning but awesomely pricey.

Government buildings, law firms and some realtors flesh out the remaining downtown scene. While busy during the day, George Town is virtually a ghost town at night, surrendering its customers to the nearby hotel strip of Seven Mile Beach.

Lots of marine experiences occur right along this waterfront including some touted snorkeling spots, SNUBA and scuba dives in the caverns, spurs and grooves. Dive boats also pick up passengers and whisk them to nearby West Bay for a dive or two.

Seven Mile Beach is also a contractor's delight, with all the top name hotels like The Ritz, more time-share and personal condos adorned in satellite dishes than you can shake a stick at, and a good variety of those staple mini-malls. These then all give way to the urban areas of the less-developed shorelines and inner neighborhoods.

Low cost attractions include a modest historical walking tour which takes in the remains of the late-18th century Fort George and the Cayman Islands National Museum, situated in the town's oldest building. The museum features changing exhibits on the islands' human and natural history. The National Art Center is also located along the waterfront and has some eclectic visual displays in its cozy but functional ground floor facility at Harbour Center.

Diving in the Cayman Islands

Loading tanks at East End

Grand Cayman visitors can choose from a wonderland of more than 120 dive sites – almost all marked with moorings and having their own distinct features and attractions. The Sister Islands have roughly 80 marked sites. It's all here: steep, deep walls adorned with sponges and corals in a stunning array of sizes and colors; shallow reefs filled with schooling and solitary fish and small invertebrates; and wrecks featuring photogenic structures and curious residents. There's also the 'world's best 12 foot dive' – the unique **Stingray City**.

Diving here usually entails one of two types of diving, a deep outer reef wall dive or a shallower inner reef dive. The deep mooring may start anywhere between 40ft and 70ft, normally atop a large coral spur. Much of the reef is what is known as a spur-and-groove system, where the undersea terrain is a series of perpendicular coral-covered fingers separated by sandy channels. These various formations can create high canyon-like walls along the sandy channels, coral-covered arches and tunnels called swim-throughs. All lead out to a vertical or steeply sloping outer wall that runs parallel to the shoreline.

A typical morning dive would be a visit to a deeper site and an exploration of the deep grooves and outer reef wall, where large sponges, diverse corals, large fish and ocean-going (pelagic) creatures can be seen. These dives tend to be short due to the short bottom time allowed for deeper depths.

The second dive would be much shallower, perhaps with a maximum depth of 35ft to 60ft, and much closer to shore. These dives allow more time to explore smaller reef life, schooling fish and most of the island's shipwrecks, and last close to an hour. A surface interval between the two dives may be as short as 40 minutes or as long as an hour. A large majority of dive sites are in West Bay, where travel time between dives is generally only 10 to 15 minutes. The popular East End and northern dive sites may take longer to reach and travel between.

Many dive shops offer 'dive 'til you drop' schedules, with two morning dives, a bit of time for lunch and then two afternoon dives. You can also do a night dive on top of all that. Others offer two morning and one afternoon dives, while a few have a boat dive and unlimited shore dive program.

Note that most, if not all, Cayman dive operations are 100% computer-based. This means every diver must have and use a computer as opposed to using the tables. Computers are available for rent and sale at Cayman dive shops. Solo diving may not be condoned by your dive operation even if you have certification; check in advance if you're a solo photographer or lone barracuda type of diver.

Grand Cayman's reefs offer a variety of Caribbean marine life encounters in extremely clear water. Spearfishing is kept to a minimum and can only be practiced by adult residents with a license. Thus, many of the fish and critters are unafraid of divers. Big fish like tarpon are normally easy to approach,

The Best Dives

Wreck Dive

The **Oro Verde** is one of the nicest dives in the Caribbean with resident angelfish and a pretty reef area. On The Sister Islands, try the *Keith Tibbets*, a Russian trawler.

Oro Verde

Wall Dive

The North Wall has lots of interesting spots including **Ghost Mountain** and **Babylon.** The **Great Wall** in Little Cayman is famous for its sheer face which starts in shallow depths and plummets to an abyss.

Reef Dive

Sunset Reef has lots to offer, including a healthy house reef with masses of macro action, a full-blown bronze mermaid statue and a small shipwreck.

Shore Dive

Turtle Reef, in front of the Cracked Conch restaurant and near the brand new turtle farm, has a mini-wall and a tarpon cave. It's nice with a full Caribbean moon as well.

Critter Dive

Stingray City has room for a lot of bottom time. You really can't ignore the stingrays and you can also explore the scattered corals heads in and around Stingray City's sandy flats for some interesting juvenile fish life.

Southern stingray

Divers prepare their own tanks and BCs

sea turtles do their thing and the sting-rays, of course, actually come to you … at least at **Stingray City**. Underwater photographers will appreciate the clarity and warmth of the sea here.

The average water temperature is between 77ºF and 83ºF degrees; average visibility is an amazing 100ft year-round, though it can increase in the summer to 200ft and fall in the winter to around 75ft.

Most Cayman Islands' hotels have an affiliated dive shop. The majority of divers stay on Grand Cayman, which has a huge diversity of sites plus a number of other entertainment options and dining amenities. Recommended shops belong to the Cayman Islands Watersports Operators Association.

WHEN TO GO

The Cayman Islands are open for diving all year. Due to the large number of dive sites all around the island, there is always a protected place to dive. It can tend to be a bit windy October into December, closing out some sites. But there are also some bargains in this low season atmosphere from September through December. From mid-December into April things can be quite busy so advance planning is necessary. The rainy season is considered May to October but rain is sporadic, not constant. March and April are the driest and calmest months. There is little in the way of cold temperatures, so this is not really a factor.

WHAT TO BRING

The Cayman Islands' climate is best described as tropical, so dress casually. The outside temperature ranges from about 70ºF to 85ºF. The hottest months are July and August and the coolest is February. It can be a bit windy in November and December and rains more during the period from May to October than during the rest of the year. March and April are the driest months.

So for almost everything, it's island casual with shorts and T-shirt by day and light, casual dress for dinner. A light jacket or sweater is about all that's needed during the cooler or windier months. It may actually be cooler in restaurants and movie theaters than outdoors in the evenings. A few of the nicer or more traditional hotels have dress codes, so check this with the hotel you are staying at.

It is okay to dress in swimwear on the dive boats and along the beaches. If going into town, visitors are asked to dress modestly and cover skimpy swimwear with beach cover-ups or shorts and T-shirts.

WHAT TO BRING DIVING

The Cayman Islands is a good place to go for a dive trip because if you do forget something, there are many fully-equipped dive shops on the island that offer both rental and sales, parts purchase and even regulator repair. If you're not picky and don't want to carry dive gear, full rental of all kit is also available at most dive shops.

The warm Caribbean sea water is tropical and clear. There are no thermoclimes as you go deeper, so water temperatures are fairly consistent at 78ºF to 84ºF (25.6°C to 28.9°C). All that is needed is a 1.5mm to 3mm wetsuit to be comfortable. Heartier folks just wear skins or T-shirts, while those acclimated, like divemasters, wear 5mm to 7mm.

Green sea turtle

Five Great Snorkeling Sites

1 **Stingray City** – This site can't be beaten for stingrays and lots of other fish in clear, blue water.
2 **SeaFans Reef** – Easy pier entry, beautiful corals and big fish make this a fascinating spot.
3 **Eden Rock** – Look for caverns, bait-fish schools and silvery tarpon at this George Town site.
4 **Sunset Reef East** – This East End site has some nice aqua waters and offers the chance to see big turtles.
5 **MV Capt. Keith Tibbetts** – The Russian wreck on the Brac's north side is a unique underwater site.

Normal scuba gear or snorkeling gear is fine for the Cayman Islands. Shore diving is common and fun in the Cayman Islands and is sometimes the best way to see certain sites. Make sure you have good booties for entering and exiting the water across a reef or rocky beach. The good news is that virtually all of the popular beach entries can be done in a giant stride from a pier or cement pier area built into the ironshore (rocky limestone shoreline). The same venues have exit ladders. So if you do like to use full foot fins, booties aren't a necessity.

Do NOT bring a speargun – they are illegal for tourists and fines are astronomical. If you try to use one and get caught (highly likely), the fines are very stiff and you will probably have to leave the Cayman Islands. Bring a camera instead. You can also leave your gloves at home. While not a rule, most divers and dive operations frown on divers using gloves. They aren't really necessary.

Don't forget your 'C' card and dive log to show your host dive shop. Nitrox is offered almost everywhere, so bring your mixed gas card if you are going to use it. Rebreather diving, rental and training is also available in the Cayman Islands.

DIVE TRAINING & CERTIFICATION

Dive operators in the Cayman Islands offer all levels of training from snorkeling and basic scuba to full instructor courses.

PADI is the main agency represented on the island, but TDI technical diving courses are also offered. Check with your dive shop to see what courses you can take. The Cayman Islands is the perfect spot for Nitrox, wreck certification, marine-life courses and many other specialties.

Diving costs are pretty much the same across the islands. Remember, the cheapest package may or may not be the best and safest training. Ask questions and shop for the best situation for your needs.

Detailed maps and briefings are normally standard practice in the Caymans.

Entrance To
EDEN ROCK

Eden Rock is one of George Town's
popular shore dives and snorkel spots

Examining a vacant conch shell

TECH DIVING

There is only one full-service tech facility on Grand Cayman, the aptly named DiveTech, although many others do offer Nitrox. DiveTech is meticulous in its gas mixes and offers technical training both at Turtle Reef and Cobalt Coast shops. It offers technical courses through the IANTD and TDI training curriculums.

Technical diving is, simply put, going beyond the recreational limits of diving. Want to dive to 130ft and stay for 45 minutes? Then tech dive training should be on your agenda. Tech training can include a gradated course starting with the use of twin/double tanks, side mounts and multi-level decompression stops. The courses start with Nitrox, then Advanced Nitrox and continue through the Advanced Trimix level.

During the Ice Age, the earth's water levels were some 200ft shallower than

they are today. This makes for some very interesting underwater topography on Grand Cayman's walls. Overhangs, where the surf used to break on the shoreline, create the perfect home for massive sponges, and chutes cut into the wall where runoff created erosion. This type of advanced, extended range of diving is not for everyone. It requires a commitment to safe, responsible, self-disciplined diving. A lot of training and practice and a little bit of an adventurous spirit also help. If this is for you, the deep world of the Caymans can be a spectacularly beautiful sight.

LIVE ABOARDS

Two live aboards are currently operating around Cayman Islands. Divers on these get to explore the walls and shipwrecks of Grand Cayman, and weather permitting, Little Cayman and Cayman Brac.

Cayman resident pro Cathy Church displays her newest book

Cathy Church is a legendary name in underwater photography and instruction, and is recognized as one of the world's foremost teachers and authors on underwater photography. She has been photographing underwater since 1967, holds a Masters Degree in Marine Biology and has received numerous awards over the years. She is on the founding board of governors of the newly established International Scuba Diving Hall of Fame, to be housed in the Cayman Islands, and was inducted into the Women Divers Hall of Fame in March 2000. She was also admitted to be a member of the Explorers' Club in 2000.

If you're heading to Grand Cayman and want to learn about underwater photography or need some coaching, Cathy offers private lessons through Cathy Church's Underwater Photo Center and Gallery at Sunset House Hotel, and has selected some great venues around Grand Cayman as her 'studio' in the sea.

Cathy is currently dabbling in black and white imagery and is considered a digital pro. Her coffee table book *My Underwater Photo Journey* was published in 2004.

SNORKELING

As the water here is very clear and bathtub warm, shore access is easy and the currents are normally mild, snorkeling is a very popular pastime. Many people come to Cayman Islands for the snorkeling alone. Remember, it is close to the equator. Wear a rash guard and some good waterproof sunscreen. It is very easy to get burned, even after just half an hour in the water.

Reef snorkels offer a look at juvenile fish, sessile invertebrates and perhaps a passing ray or sea turtle, while the mangroves are a fascinating web of roots and provide a completely different ecosystem than the reef world. The rocky limestone shoreline, called the ironshore, also offers a look at the tidal world where you can snorkel or reef walk and see small eels, crabs, urchins, anemones and lots more. If you've never tried snorkeling, the Caymans are a superb place to do it. If you want to see extreme snorkeling, world-record deep diving competitions using breath-hold only diving are held here annually.

UNDERWATER PHOTOGRAPHY

Underwater photography is a favored activity for many divers traveling to the Cayman Islands. Less particles in the water increases the water clarity as well as the number of good images a photographer can create in a dive. The brilliant orange elephant ear sponges, schools of chromis, ever-hungry stingrays and roaming lobsters make this a diving photographer's delight. The marine diversity and unique topography make the Cayman Islands a great place for colorful wide angle lens work, medium focal length for fish and macro photos alike.

Most of the larger dive centers provide camera rental or have a staff pro who can provide instruction or shoot a personal video. E-6 slide processing

A southern stingray approaches a photographer

A snapper gets up close and personal

In the Cayman Islands, most good dive boats have a camera table of some sort and a fresh water bucket that can hold around three housed point-and-shoot cameras and strobes (or one SLR system). If you want your own freshwater rinse, it may be best to head to Foster's or one of the main stores and buy a cooler big enough for your SLR to use for your dive week.

On land, the tanks dedicated to camera rinse can be rather crowded with both boat and shore divers all sharing the same bin. In some cases, masks and fins are allowed to be washed in the same water. Few operations have large specifically dedicated camera-only rinse tanks. As most divers use wrist lanyards, a crowded rinse bin and boat rinse tub can result in other users hastily pulling their gear out and snagging yours as well. This can cause latches to unlock and uncovered domes and ports to get scratched. While it seems like a good idea to keep your camera wet all the time, the lack of boat basins and the overcrowding at the shop can become a problem. Better to keep your camera wet with a damp towel on board and then soak it in your hotel room's bathtub.

Also, be warned that the sand here is very fine at most beaches. Since beach diving is a major part of the dive scene, entries in and out of surf zones with a lot of fine sand in the water can be harmful to the health of your camera. Even if you are going up a ladder at the ironshore (rocky limestone shoreline), that shallow surf zone is pretty well full of tiny sand particles floating around. After beach dives, carefully check and clean your o-rings to ensure fine sand particles have not gotten lodged in the o-ring slots and on the rings themselves. A little preventive maintenance in the evenings can be worth many dollars in replacing a camera due to a flooded housing from an errant speck of beach sand.

is becoming harder to find as digital takes over the photo scene by leaps and bounds. Ask if your dive center or live aboard offers it before you go if you want on-the-spot results. Print film is still processed commercially.

The main camera store in town is The Camera Store in the Waterfront Centre on the main drive across from the new cruise ship terminal in George Town. It offers a large selection of digital cameras, lenses, print film processing and printing, camcorders and lots of accessories and digital media. Cathy Church's Underwater Photo Centre at the Sunset House Hotel also offers a nice array of gear and housings, plus instruction from Cathy or Herb Rafael.

Doing boat dives and especially shore dives with a good Cayman Islands underwater photographer is highly recommended, as they can point out habitat and find that elusive fish, like the ever photogenic pike blenny.

A seaside view to the North Sound

Conservation

Cayman's rich inner lagoon and mangroves

There is a great deal of value placed upon the preservation of coral reefs around the islands, which is reflected in the section of the law which makes it an offence for anyone without a license to cut, carve, injure, mutilate, displace or break any underwater corals, plant growth or formations. Few divers need to be reminded not to break off a piece of coral to take home as a souvenir of their Cayman vacation. Many, if not most, corals grow at a rate of less than half an inch a year, so if the underwater beauty that has taken centuries to develop is to remain for the future enjoyment of everyone in Cayman, residents and visitors must act responsibly.

Also prohibited is the use of spearguns (including the Hawaiian sling, pole spear, harpoon, hookstick or any device with a pointed end which may be used to impale, stab or pierce any marine life) or seine nets without a license from the Marine Conservation Board. Only Caymanians over 18 may be granted these licenses.

There is also a movement to prevent the establishment of any captive dolphin training centers and exhibits. Shark feeding is also illegal.

The Environmental Zone, Marine Parks and Replenishment Zones are all clearly marked around the islands by distinctive orange and white spar buoys. Dive sites are buoyed by one of two sizes of white buoys with a blue band surrounding them – the majority are single pin moorings installed in an environmentally friendly manner by the Department of Environment.

Signs giving information about marine conservation laws and regulations are located on the shores of most marine parks, and leaflets, laminated maps and stickers are also available. For more information, contact the Department of Environment (☎ 949 8469; Channel 17 on the marine VHF; PO Box 486GT).

Coral Facts by Dee Scarr

Sponge covered overhang in West Bay

The facts of life for coral:

1 Be aware that we use the word 'coral' for three things: the individual coral animal, called the polyp; the polyps and the skeleton they've secreted, also called a coral head; and the skeleton without its living polyps, also called coral rock. The first two of these are alive, while the last is not alive, which leaves a great deal of room for confusion.

2 A coral polyp (the living coral animal) is only three to four cell layers thick.

3 To create a model of coral tissue against its own skeleton, take a wet tissue and drape it across a bare razorblade.

4 Every individual coral animal in a coral head is a clone of every other coral animal in that coral head.

5 A coral head is started by a single coral larva which grows and begins to secrete a calcium-based skeleton, then clones itself, and repeats the process. Slowly.

6 A hemispherical coral head of 3ft diameter is two- to three-hundred years old.

7 The branching corals, elkhorn and staghorn, grow more quickly than the 'head' corals, such as brain and star coral. They thrive in shallower waters, so are more likely to be broken by wave action.

8 Look at a star coral head, or a starlet coral head. Every single little mound or indentation – every single little circle in the whole coral head – is an individual coral animal.

9 Look at a brain coral head, or a sheet coral. The polyps aren't as easy to distinguish as they are in the star corals, but a careful look will reveal the mouths of the polyps, day or night.

10 The tissue of every coral polyp in a coral head is connected to all the polyps around it. The entire surface of a coral head is covered with living coral tissue.

CORAL

Coral is perhaps the most important component of the Cayman Island's reef system. There are two distinct groups of corals: hard and soft. Hard or stony corals make up the majority of reef building creatures that are responsible for laying down the structure of the reef. While they may look like rocks, they are in fact colonies of tiny delicate animals called polyps, which grow by laying down a stony skeleton. Soft corals include the sea fans, sea whips, sea feather plumes and sea rods. Like their close relatives the stony corals, soft corals also possess tiny polyps, grow very slowly and are extremely delicate. Marine Conservation laws make it an offense to damage coral by anchoring in it or close to it. It is also illegal to collect coral while on scuba anywhere in the Cayman Islands.

Expensive Piece of Fish

It is vital that any successful marine parks management plan adopts adequate surveillance and enforcement. The Cayman Islands currently has three marine parks enforcement officers operating under the Department of Environment to patrol the waters of the marine parks. Since there are so many boats on the water daily, local captains also help form a network to report an infringement that may be observed. Poaching is considered a serious offense and is not taken lightly. Stiff penalties are in place to deal with offenders; the maximum fine of CI$500,000 (about US$595,000), one year in jail and confiscation of boats and equipment is a pretty expensive price to pay for a piece of fish.

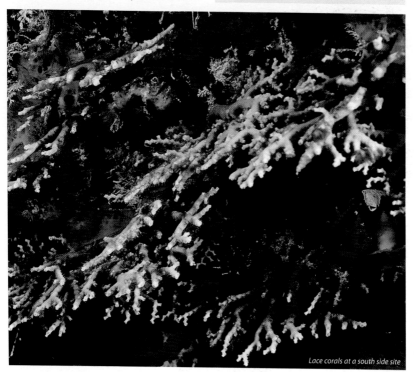

Lace corals at a south side site

Health & Safety

A Grand Cayman policeman directs tourist traffic

Overall, the Cayman Islands is a healthy destination to visit. There are no exotic diseases and the mosquito bites lead only to itching.

The main island has hospitals, a number of practicing doctors, and an ambulance plane on call for emergencies. George Town Hospital (Hospital Rd, George Town, Cayman Islands; ☎ (345) 949-8600) is the largest hospital in the Cayman Islands. It has surgical, maternity, pediatric and emergency units. A dental clinic, eye clinic and pharmacy are also found here. Due to the popularity of diving, the hospital also has a two-man decompression chamber. Ambulance paramedic services are available 24 hours by dialing ☎ 911 or

☎ 555. The main number is ☎ (345) 949-8600. Lilith McLaughlin Memorial Health Center in East End, Dica Brown Memorial Health Center in North Side and the West Bay Nurses Health Center also provide health services.

Chrissie Tomlinson Memorial Hospital (☎ (345) 945-1695) is a private outpatient/inpatient specialist hospital, also on Hospital Road close to the George Town Hospital. It has 18 beds, including a 24-hour urgent care and injury center, medical laboratory and pharmacy. It is open to the public as well. Contact: ☎ (345) 945-1695.

Faith Hospital is a small facility on Cayman Brac, and there is a satellite clinic on Little Cayman.

Rating System for Dives & Divers

A giant stride makes for easy shore diving

The dive sites in this book are rated according to divers at a particular time, diving at a particular place. These are not absolute ratings. For instance, someone unfamiliar with prevailing conditions might be considered a novice diver at one dive area, but an intermediate diver at another, more familiar location.

Novice:
A novice diver generally fits the following profile:
- basic scuba certification from an internationally recognized certifying agency
- dives infrequently (less than one trip a year)
- logged fewer than 25 total dives
- little or no experience diving in similar waters and conditions
- dives no deeper than 60ft (18m).

*An instructor or divemaster should accompany a novice diver on all dives.

Intermediate:
An intermediate diver generally fits the following profile:
- may have participated in some form of continuing diver education
- logged between 25 and 100 dives
- no deeper than 130ft (40m)
- has been diving within the last six months in similar waters and conditions.

Advanced:
An advanced diver generally fits the following profile:
- advanced certification
- has been diving for more than two years; logged over 100 dives
- has been diving within the last six months in similar waters and conditions.

Pre-dive Safety Guidelines
Regardless of skill level, you should be in good physical condition and know your limitations. If you are uncertain as to which category you fit, ask the advice of a local dive instructor. He or she is best qualified to assess your abilities based on the prevailing dive conditions at any given site. Ultimately, you must decide if you are capable of making a particular dive, depending on your level of training, recent experience and physical condition, as well as water conditions at the site. Remember that water conditions can change at any time, even during a dive.

Island time in the Caymans

PRE-TRIP PREPARATION

Shops in the Cayman Islands offer equipment for sale and rental, and also equipment repair. If you are using your own gear, get your regulator tuned up before leaving home if you haven't used it for over six months. You may also want to do some local check-out dives, even if just in a pool.

It's worth exercising prior to the trip in order to face the challenges of boat diving and the ins and outs and walks associated with shore diving. Swimming, hiking with a backpack and jogging will help increase fitness and stamina.

Make sure your passport is not about to expire or hasn't already expired. You can't get into the Cayman Islands without one and you can't get back home even if you do manage to get in.

Cayman guides take great pride in dive mapping

MEDICAL & RECOMPRESSION FACILITIES

It is highly recommended that you take out DAN or some sort of medical insurance prior to a dive vacation. Some dive operations now make it mandatory. Divers should consult with their medical insurance company prior to traveling abroad to confirm whether the policy applies overseas and covers emergency expenses such as a medical evacuation.

Grand Cayman has a recompression chamber in George Town Hospital staffed by physicians and technical staff familiar with diving medicine. There are no chambers in the outer islands.

Your DAN affiliate should also be consulted in the event of a diving accident, or diving illness symptoms, as well as your dive shop manager so they can react to the emergency and set things in motion for treatment. There is a system in the Caymans to get bent divers proper treatment. If you think you have a problem, don't mess around. Contact the dive shop, boat captain and DAN immediately.

Cayman Hyperbaric Services
☎ (345) 949-2989; email diveraid@candw.ky; PO Box 1675GT, Grand Cayman, B.W.I; George Town Hospital. Chamber Director John Elliott CHT (☎ (345) 916 1198).

George Town Hospital
☎ (345) 949-8600 ext 2795) Doctors: Dr Fiona Robinson, Dr Robin Barnes and Dr Denise Osterloh.

DAN

Divers Alert Network (DAN) is an international membership association of individuals and organizations sharing a common interest in diving and safety. The network operates a 24-hour diving emergency hotline in the US at ☎ 919-684-8111 or ☎ 919-684-4DAN (which accepts collect calls in a dive emergency). DAN does not directly provide medical care; however, it does provide advice on early treatment, evacuation, and hyperbaric treatment of diving-related injuries.

All divers should have DAN or some similar insurance. Some dive companies and live aboards do actually require it, so take care of your diving insurance before you head to the Cayman Islands to avoid problems.

An aerial view of North Sound and Sandbar

North Wall & North Sound

A stingray comes to greet divers

This area is home to several famous shallow and deep dives. **Stingray City** and **Sandbar** inside the North Channel in the northwest end of the vast North Sound lagoon are the best known sites by far, where huge stingrays have become accustomed to divers, snorkelers and waders, and never fail to thrill.

But the entirety of North Sound is one of the island's finest assets. It's a huge, natural incubation site for all kinds of waterfowl, marine plants, juvenile fish and invertebrates, and sites outside the main channel benefit greatly from this treasure trove.

The wall outside the Sound area is alive with marine life of all sorts, where deep grooves and coral encrusted drop-offs provide a multitude of shelter types for huge fish, shoals of colorful tropicals and flurries of tiny reef fish.

Considered by many to be the island's premier place to explore, the dives here, when accessible, are always promising.

North Wall & North Sound	GOOD SNORKELING	NOVICE	INTERMEDIATE	ADVANCED
1 STINGRAY CITY	•	•		
2 SANDBAR	•	•		
3 LESLIE'S CURL	•	•		
4 EAGLE RAY PASS	•		•	
5 PRINCESS PENNY'S PINNACLE	•		•	
6 TARPON ALLEY	•		•	
7 HOLE IN THE WALL	•		•	
8 GHOST MOUNTAIN	•		•	
9 COBALT RIDGE	•		•	
10 SEA FANS 1 THRU 3	•		•	

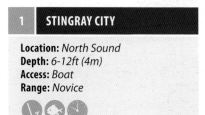

1 STINGRAY CITY

Location: *North Sound*
Depth: *6-12ft (4m)*
Access: *Boat*
Range: *Novice*

One of the world's most famous dives, Stingray City is fun, shallow and located in a beautiful setting.

The dive starts with an on-board briefing about how to settle on the bottom and interact with the stingrays. The lecture normally contains some stingray info as well, so you learn a bit about these amazing creatures.

While this is mainly a shallow dive site, people snorkel above the feeders to watch the action. The water is normally crystal clear, making it easy to see what's going on. Ray wranglers may even swim up with a ray or two following, to give snorkelers a good, close look.

Upon descending, hungry rays will probably already be near the boat. If not, it is a thrilling sight to see a group of anywhere from four to 14 stingrays winding their way toward you across the snow white sand. Rays here have been measured at over 4ft across and weighing over 125 pounds. There have been reports of 6ft rays, however this far exceeds their normal adult size. Still, there are definitely some big ones.

Stingray City's Stingrays

Stingray City

It is estimated that between 3,000 and 5,000 people visit the stingray attractions in the Grand Cayman North Sound on every day that weather permits. Many of these visitors are from cruise ships, while others are divers and snorkelers staying on the island. In any case, from mid-morning through to the early afternoon, it's a busy place.

The rays found here are called southern stingrays. As the story goes, the cut in the reef which leads to this area of the North Sound was a popular one for fishermen to enter and then sit in calm water within the Main Channel while cleaning the day's catch. As they threw the bones and guts overboard, rays learned about this spot and came to feed on the discarded fish parts. Eventually word got out to divers, and it quickly became a dive attraction.

The fishermen are all but gone nowadays, but the rays remain. In the wild, they aren't normally seen flying across the reef as they do here, preferring to usually keep buried in the sand. With their eyes set high on their body, they can rest in this camouflaged state whilst keeping an eye out for predators, such as Caribbean reef sharks or hammerheads.

Rays also have one or more serrated, venomous sheathed barbs, four to eight inches long, that can be used to ward off enemies or someone settling on top of them These can inflict a painful wound in humans which may quickly become infected, and if the barb breaks off, it must be surgically removed.

When hungry, rays can be seen foraging through the sand, often in the company of a bar jack or a goatfish which will try to grab any morsel the ray may scare up or leave behind. Rays eat small fish, clams, crabs, lobsters and other invertebrates, and their powerful jaws can crush shellfish and crustaceans easily.

Reports of stings and accidents at the Cayman's popular sites, such as Stingray City and **Sandbar** are actually very rare. The rays here have become quite tame and used to humans. Still, they are wild creatures and care should be taken not to handle, grab or step on them.

Rays also have a protective mucous on their skins. Touching them can remove this coating, leaving them vulnerable to infection. Look but don't touch – leave that to the ray wranglers, who know what they're doing.

There can be some current at this site as it's close to the Main Channel, so extra weight can be helpful, plus it helps anchor you in place to watch rays feed without having to deal with buoyancy issues.

Try to find a nice sandy spot and settle down with the other divers in a circle around your ray wrangler. Divemasters usually have a canister containing squid which the rays come in to eat, although this is not their normal fare in the wild. Wranglers release bits of squid at intervals with a few waves of the canister, keeping the rays around for you to watch and interact with.

This can go on for quite a while, especially if no other boat comes around. Dives typically last over an hour, and since it is only about 15ft deep if you use a shovel, it's rare to use an entire tank here. Rays can be fickle though, and may disperse when a new group shows up, but often they or another group will return.

Rays aren't the only fish to be seen here. The ubiquitous yellowtail snappers are always present, and there are also a couple of large groupers and a large, somewhat cataract-affected green moray eel. This eel can't see well,

so if it does put in an appearance, keep your hands close to your body. There are also some great barracuda lurking about. If any of these guys show up, the wrangler may cease feeding for a while, as they can strike like lightning.

It may seem incongruous to bring a macro lens on this dive, but the site is very close to a reef channel and also an outlet for the mangroves in the inner bay. There is some very good small marine life at the many coral heads near the anchorage. About a half-hour into the dive, the divemaster may stop ray feeding to lead a short tour through the corals and coral heads. Look here for juvenile blue tang, lobsters large and small, juvenile spotted drums, red reef shrimp, flame scallops, juvenile angelfish, anemones with Pederson anemone shrimp and lots of other small creatures that may have developed in the mangroves and are now heading out for a life on the reef. Even seahorses can pop up here.

The feeding will then often continue at the end of the reef tour. Enjoy the rays and this amazing interaction, as there are few places like it in the world. Many divers come back for second and third dives here, as it's always fun and great for photos.

The beautiful stingrays at Stingray City in black and white

2   SANDBAR

Location: *North Sound, east of Stingray City*
Depth: *0-5ft (1.5m)*
Access: *Boat*
Range: *Novice, snorkel only*

This site is more for non-divers who still want to see stingrays. A popular wading and snorkeling spot about two miles east of **Stingray City,** the procedure here is much the same as in Stingray City. A designated feeder uses a canister of squid pieces to lure rays in to be fed, while visitors get to watch as the rays zip in.

Research has found that these rays are mostly females (normally the larger ones) and that they hang around to be fed by day. Males tend to stay farther away from the site, but they must get together sometime, as many of the rays here will often be pregnant.

Tube sponges at Leslie's Curl

It was also found that the fed rays remained at the Sandbar during the day. They do leave the area a little at night, probably to find crustaceans if still hungry, but they then return the next morning and await feeding time.

These rays should not be lifted out of the water or grabbed – simply enjoy watching their graceful movements whilst taking part in one of diving's unique interactions.

3   LESLIE'S CURL

Location: *North Wall*
Depth: *60-100ft (18-30m)*
Access: *Boat*
Range: *Novice*

This site starts rather deep, which is pretty much the norm for most of the wall area northwest of the Main Channel. A deep spur and groove system, there are nice cuts with sandy bottoms and healthy corals around 75ft to 85ft. A feature known as the curl is an undercut in the main outer wall at around 75ft. Swim from the mooring eye straight out and over the wall to see it. Inside there are growths of black coral, plus tunicates and ascidian colonies.

This area is known for big fish, so keep an eye out for large groupers. Out in the blue there's a chance of seeing Caribbean reef sharks, sea turtles and eagle rays. Just remember that this is a deep dive, so bottom time will be rather short.

Purple sea fans, sea whips and lacey gorgonians thrive here, and beautiful purple-tipped sea anemones with Pederson shrimp can also be found. Shallow depths are good for turtles, as well as green morays that like the cracks along the reeftop.

Keep an eye on your air during this dive as it starts rather deep, where the tendency is to burn air more quickly.

A divemaster or ray wrangler
steers a ray toward nearby divers

Photographing Stingrays at Stingray City

When one sees stingrays in the wild, they are normally buried in the sand or creating clouds of sand while foraging for a meal. If this is the case, approach low and slow, breathing very lightly and making slow movements. Try to expose for the ambient light and just fill the image with your strobe, as the light sand can be very reflective.

If you're at Stingray City though, the rules can change as the rays will often be swimming up at camera level and even above your head. While they have gray to tan bodies, their white bellies are quite reflective, so exposing for both is tough. The site is also primarily white, fine sand, but this is a plus, as the ambient light reflected from the sand helps fill and light everyone in the scene.

Do you need strobes in such a shallow setting? In a word, yes. The color red starts to disappear as shallow as 5ft to 8ft, but the strobe restores proper color. The site is usually pretty bright, so it is best to just use strobes here as fill light to maintain color. Meter on something light gray (or even use the back of a stingray), take a few shots to see how the exposure is and adjust accordingly. The lowest power on the strobe will act as fill and also not reflect as much from sand as a higher one.

Of course, if you want to try for a ray swimming past a big sunburst, this all changes to higher settings and f-stops. But for over reef scenes and feeding photos, just meter the scene, expose for it and fill with low strobe power.

Another method involves no strobes at all. There are filters designed to be used with your digital white balance that add the red spectrum and allow for a normal exposure. If shot very close to the surface, they can leave a slight red or pinkish hue, but shot down around 12ft they are fine. Just remember to keep the sun at your back.

Stingray City is an action-packed dive site that is good for many clicks of the shutter. Have fun.

4 EAGLE RAY PASS

Location: *North Wall*
Depth: *42-100ft (16-30m)*
Access: *Boat*
Range: *Intermediate*

The likelihood of seeing an eagle ray, or even a whole school of them, is good on this dive. Eagle rays have a tendency to be rather shy and don't like being approached, so if you see one, get down low on the reef and breathe lightly. When not intimidated, they can also be curious. If you are near the sandy shallower part of this dive, act like you're looking for something in the sand, as these rays may think you're feeding and come to join you.

Situated west of **Leslie's Curl** in the middle of the Main Channel, this site is a good place to see pelagic creatures swimming in the channel's outflow and intake. As scalloped hammerheads, blacktips and Caribbean reef sharks all like to eat stingrays, these may also be seen cruising here, looking to nab a foraging stingray or even an eagle ray.

This is a stunning site with a large sand chute and canyon-like walls on the side. At one point the sides nearly converge, forming a near arch. At about 70ft the chute spills out to the wall, and the dive can become a search for both Mr Big in the blue and Mr Small on the wall. Large barrel sponges, lacey gorgonians, healthy plate corals and a smattering of sea anemones adorn this wall, while the cracks and crannies are home to green morays, spiny lobsters and queen angelfish.

On the way back up, check out the canyons on either side of the chute for more good marine life. This site isn't as deep as **Leslie's Curl,** with a sandy area about 40ft deep up top, but the wall can be bottomless, so watch your air and depth here nevertheless.

5 PRINCESS PENNY'S PINNACLE

Location: *North Wall*
Depth: *45-130ft (14-30m)*
Access: *Boat*
Range: *Intermediate*

This site was named after Penny Ventura, who was a world class free diver. Princess Penny's Pinnacle is a great site with a lot going on. It has a stunning wall with lots of coral and marine life, including cleaning stations with banded coral shrimp, anemones with commensal shrimp and crabs and huge sponges.

Distinguishing features include swim-throughs and a pinnacle off the main wall. The pinnacle can be seen from the mooring as you descend, and is decorated by large deepwater gorgonians with clouds of fish swarming over the top. Creole wrasse fill out the water column, as do black durgons. Other fish life includes yellowtail snappers, large triggerfish and shy queen angelfish. Look too for cleaning stations in and around the beautiful large barrel sponges.

The wall is also worth a good look. Swim through the narrow, chimneylike passage west of the mooring, which spits you out on the wall at 75ft. Tube, rope and finger sponges cover the wall and large plate corals hold habitat for gobies. This is also a good place to see eagle rays and perhaps a foraging hawksbill. Swim a bit to the east and there is another chimney at 90ft that leads up to reeftop at 45ft.

The North Sound

While the rays garner most of the attention in the North Sound bay area, which takes up most of central and northwest Grand Cayman, birdlife, marine plants and fish all thrive in its protected and nurturing environment. Sports enthusiasts are also attracted to certain portions of this bay, for kite surfing, kayaking and some major snorkeling.

Mangroves line a good portion of the inner bay and there are even some small cayes. Mangroves are a highly important incubation area for many reef species, both fish and invertebrate, providing shelter and a food supply for juveniles, including spiny lobsters and various grunts and snappers that later move to the reefs. The mangroves' tangled root systems absorb and disperse wave energy, preventing extensive erosion or flooding problems. They also provide a buffer that protects reefs from nutrient-rich sediment loads washed into the sea.

If you look closely you'll see a very complex eco-system here. A helicopter flight over North Sound will reveal roaming reef sharks (patrolling for stingrays) on the mangrove edges, stingrays and eagle rays. Birds can also be found nesting and hunting in the area.

Many smaller creatures use the shelter provided by both the mangrove root system and the sea grasses for protection and habitat. The bay holds sea grasses, sometimes called turtle grass. Snails, juvenile fish, crabs, shrimp, juvenile lobsters and many other invertebrates live here or in the silty sand that the grass holds in place.

This is an important area for keeping Grand Cayman's reefs healthy and diverse. Enjoy these protected inland waters and if bird watching, snorkeling or kayaking here, treat the environment with great care and respect.

6 TARPON ALLEY

Location: *North Wall*
Depth: *45-130ft (14-30m)*
Access: *Boat*
Range: *Intermediate*

Divers can expect to see silvery tarpon here, where upwards of 50 are known to school, making for a very cool and fun dive site. The norm is to find a dozen or so here, but this can vary to larger numbers, with reports of up to 100 being seen.

Silvery tarpon are hard to miss and are sometimes even mistaken for sharks by new divers. Measuring 3ft to 6ft in length, they are quite accustomed to the presence of divers in 'The Alley' and can be photographed fairly closely. Since they are silvery, try to use a low flash power, otherwise the strobe will reflect too much and blast all the detail from the fish. This can be tricky but you'll usually get a few tries at it, as they

Schooling silver tarpon

aren't too spooky. To find them, head to the wall. Near the drop-off there is a long and narrow canyon with a sandy bottom. The fish will be in the ravine and under overhangs in this area, hovering almost motionless. Do not rush in or they will head out – approach slowly and steadily.

If you really want, you can also dive the wall here and look at the sponge and fish life; however, this site primarily gives you the opportunity to make a fairly shallow (for the North Sound) dive and enjoy some other fish life as well.

The large loaf-shaped coral here has some smaller coral heads on it and lots of fish, including parrotfish, snappers, whitespotted filefish and angels. There can also be rays in the surrounding sand, while sea fans, sponges and sea plumes adorn the reeftop.

While some places may have tarpon off and on, this site is pretty much a sure thing.

7 HOLE IN THE WALL

Location: *North Wall*
Depth: *45-130ft (14-30m)*
Access: *Boat*
Range: *Intermediate*

This is a deep dive with some rewarding sights. Another of the deeper dives here, the bottom of the mooring sits in 60ft of water. Head out to the wall where the site is marked by some pinnacles and deep cuts and crevices.

As well as being on the deeper end of the spectrum, there can also be some current here, which at times gets rather strong. This attracts schools of chromis and active Creole wrasse, and sharks and eagle rays may also appear. These, along with the corals and sponges make for a fascinating dive, even if bottom time is somewhat limited.

A stoplight parrotfish

8 GHOST MOUNTAIN

Location: *North Wall*
Depth: *45-130ft (14-30m)*
Access: *Boat*
Range: *Intermediate*

This is an eerie dive, as the 'mountain' is not usually visible when one descends the anchor line. Legend has it that back in the pre-digital days, a photographer had been shooting the site and it was only when he got his film back that the 'mountain' was seen, looming like a ghost in the background. When they went back to the site, they found this deep pinnacle.

From the mooring, head out to the wall area. There are deep grooves with nice plate coral and yellow tube sponges on either side of a large coral-covered spur. Sea plumes and sea fingers cover the reef, and the sponge life here is diverse with tube sponges, netted barrel sponges, leathery barrel sponges and branching and brown tube clusters all to be found along the way.

Then it appears like a ghost: an active pinnacle rising up to around 80ft to 90 ft, full of marine life. Creole wrasse, jacks and blue and silver chromis all move in the current, while huge groupers hang on to the plate corals that cover the pinnacle. Big lacey sea fans quiver in the current, and there is a large star coral head atop the pinnacle itself. Brown tube sponges can also be seen to adorn the top of one point where the pinnacle is undercut.

There is also a deep cave-like area and some deep grooves and spurs along the wall leading back up to the shallows. To fully appreciate the site and because of the depth, it is best to follow the guide around the first time here and get the lay of the place. A lot of the bigger and more colorful growth, plus a lot of the fish action, is at the deeper end of the dive, so be sure to watch your computer and air.

When you head back up to the mooring, the 'mountain' may again disappear from sight, like a ghost into the blue.

The tip of Ghost Mountain

Hurricane Ivan Documented

Mid-October 2004 is a time that Cayman Islands residents and long-time visitors recall with trepidation. A tropical hurricane hit the low island, killing two people, flooding virtually everything and leaving a total mess for everyone.

After the storm had passed a quarter of all buildings on the three islands were reported uninhabitable, and only 20% escaped without any sort of damage, with the damage bill totaling US$1.85 billion.

A direct hit by a big storm is an extremely rare occurrence here, and the before and after has been documented by resident photographer Courtney Platt. A contract photographer for *National Geographic,* his book brings home firsthand the damage that was caused – looking at Grand Cayman today it is hard to believe it all happened so recently.

According to Platt, 'As Hurricane Ivan approached at category 5, we all knew it was going to be a bad one, but few could have anticipated the enormity of the devastation that was left in its wake here.'

His book was made in the hope that readers will gain a better appreciation for the power of this storm and the extent of the damage it inflicted on the people and properties in Grand Cayman.

Says Platt, 'Consider that as much wreckage as you will see in the book, this still represents only a fraction of the total destruction caused by Ivan, the most grievously expensive disaster in Cayman's inhabited history.'

This book is intended to be a collector's item, as well as a reminder to all who live in harm's way to prepare properly for the next big storm. It can be purchased at island book stores and dive shops.

Sea turtle swims along the Cobalt Ridge

9 COBALT RIDGE

Location: *In front of Cobalt Coast Resort*
Depth: *30-80ft (9-26m)*
Access: *Boat*
Range: *Intermediate*

Cobalt Ridge is the upper reef portion of the deep wall that sits in front of the cozy Cobalt Coast Resort and just west of Spanish Bay. Cut and groove formations make navigation easy right from the front door of the DiveTech dive shop.

There is a very deep wall that's a 15 minute swim off shore, but the best part of this dive is closer in, along the mini-walls that run parallel to the shore and associated spurs and grooves. This is sometimes done as a boat dive, with divers then swimming back to shore where they are taken to their hotel by van, unless they're staying at Cobalt Coast, in which case they can just take off their gear and have lunch. Access to the area can also be done by rented underwater scooter or plain old swimming.

One can dive to the right or left of the Cobalt Coast pier and find a rich reef full of marine growth with lots of creatures living in the dense reef cover. This may be one of thickest areas of marine growth on the island, with small, hard coral heads littering the area. There are also stands of various sizes of sea rods and sea plumes, and purple sea fans mix in with yellow tube sponges to make the reef colorful. On the right side, a mini-wall of sorts has some very nice purple finger sponges and red encrusting sponges and plating corals cover the walls and ridges.

For fish life, look for black durgons in large numbers down deep. The corals hold neon gobies, chromis, roaming schools of Creole wrasse, red squirrelfish and fairy basslets. Gray angelfish follow hawksbill sea turtles looking for tidbits dropped by the turtle. Look too in the sandy channels for stingrays.

A truly fun dive that's not too deep if you don't attempt the wall, this is a great place for photos. If you aren't boat diving, going back up takes you through the following listed site, which is another very fishy place.

10	**SEA FANS 1 THRU 3**

Location: *In front of DiveTech Pier*
Depth: *15-35ft (4-11m)*
Access: *Boat*
Range: *Intermediate*

The Grand Cayman dive operation DiveTech has a couple of strategically-placed dive shops at two good walk-in dive venues: this one at the Cobalt Coast Hotel pier and another at the Cracked Conch restaurant at the north end of West Bay (around the point at Boatswain's Point, by the new turtle farm facility).

The three buoys out front of the dive shop at Cobalt Coast have been dubbed 'Sea Fans One thru Three'. This broad, flat reef top has some of the island's healthiest elkhorn coral growing right up to the shore. It's all very shallow, with thousands of small, swaying purple sea fans (*Gorgonia ventalina*) to be seen. There is very little sand across the reeftop, but it's a good place to watch various herbivorous fishes peck away at the sea floor looking for food.

As you get a bit deeper farther out, growths become larger and more varied. Large sea plumes, sea fingers and larger fans adorn the reeftop, and you

can find good rare macro stuff such as fingerprint cyphomas.

Mini-coral heads have just enough size to attract yellow tube sponges, sea fans, sea plumes and schooling fish. Many of the coral heads, large gorgonians and sea rod stands are also magnets for schoolmasters, grunts and blue-striped grunts. Congregations of over 500 fish have been seen here on a regular basis for years.

Since the DiveTech folks dive the area often, for both training and tours, it may pay to use one of their guides to show you some of the fishier hotspots and point out potential habitat for a creature you want to see. However, you can also do it alone and make discoveries as you swim and explore.

It is very shallow along this whole stretch of inner reef and nice, long dives can be enjoyed. Some divers come to spend the day, as the hotel restaurant overlooks the reef, enabling many dives to be easily made here and at the **Cobalt Ridge** site. Snorkelers will also enjoy this site, as the water is generally quite clear.

Snappers school in big numbers at these colorful sites

Exploring the inner world of the Doc Polson

Northwest Point & West Bay

Sunset along Cobalt Coast beach

Dives in the Northwest Point and West Bay area are numerous, due to this side normally being protected from wind and swell, allowing diving here pretty much all year around. Moorings can only have one dive boat at a time on them, so the only problem is that someone may beat you to your pre-ferred site and you'll have to settle for another site nearby. This is a good area for photographers to engage a knowl-edgeable local guide to help out with spotting macro subjects and point out reef life behavior.

Drop-offs, walls and big fish are all main attractions along the deeper dives at this scenic bay, which takes in Seven Mile Beach plus some fascinating iron-shore (rocky limestone shoreline) dives and snorkeling sites on either end of West Bay. Fish and invertebrate vari-ety here is good, with everything from eagle rays and sea turtles to squid, jaw-fish and lots of big sponges all added to the list of usual suspects to be found along the West Bay reefs. There are also some good small shipwrecks on many sites, a couple of statues and some great snorkeling venues.

Northwest Point & West Bay	GOOD SNORKELING	NOVICE	INTERMEDIATE	ADVANCED
11 TURTLE FARM	●		●	
12 NORTHWEST POINT	●		●	
13 BONNIE'S ARCH	●		●	
14 ORANGE CANYON	●		●	
15 SENTINEL ROCK	●		●	
16 BIG TUNNEL	●		●	
17 LITTLE TUNNELS	●		●	
18 ROUND ROCK			●	
19 TRINITY CAVES			●	
20 SAND CHUTE			●	
21 DOC POLSON WRECK	●		●	
22 MITCH MILLER'S	●		●	
23 AQUARIUM SOUTH & NORTH	●	●		
24 PETER'S (GOVERNOR'S) REEF	●	●		
25 ORO VERDE	●		●	
26 HAMMERHEAD HOLE	●	●		
27 CARIBBEAN SANDCHUTE	●		●	
28 RHAPSODY (MESA)	●	●		
29 ROYAL PALMS LEDGE	●	●		
30 CHEESEBURGER REEF	●	●		
31 BALBOA	●	●		
32 EDEN ROCK & DEVIL'S GROTTO	●	●		
33 DON FOSTER'S	●	●		
34 PARROT'S REEF	●	●		
35 SUNSET REEF & LCM NICHOLSON	●	●		
36 EAGLE RAY ROCK	●		●	

Cayman Turtle Farm

Hundreds of sea turtles entertain visitors

Near the dive site is the brand new Cayman turtle farm, now called 'Boatswain's Beach' (www.boatswainsbeach.ky). It is the only one of its kind in the world. This operation raises green turtles for purposes both benign – increasing their population in the wild – and slightly more base – selling their meat and shells. It is located across the street from the storm-ravaged remnants of the old facility.

The new and improved complex is huge, with wild iguanas running around, a plethora of turtle tanks, a Caiman croc, a bird aviary, nature trail and snorkel lagoon. With a restaurant and gift shop, it is intended as a place where people can spend a whole day.

Visitors can see and hold turtles which are hatched and raised in captivity here for conservation, research, education and utilization. This is why you'll see local restaurants on the island selling turtle steaks and turtle soup – it's all farm-raised turtle meat. Turtles of different ages are on display, ranging from newly-hatched animals to adults, with some breeders possibly over 100 years old. During summer the artificial nesting beach shows signs of sea turtle nesting and the hatchery displays all the stages of hatchling development.

A popular addition is the Predator Tank, which showcases sharks and large predatory fish to be found around the Caymans. Sharks on display include sandbar and nurse sharks, while fishes include tarpon and jacks. These predators can be viewed from above, from underwater in the boatswain's lagoon and from inside the freshwater swimming pool through gigantic 4in thick acrylic windows. During feeding time visitors can see sharks feeding just a few feet off the main viewing window.

11   TURTLE FARM

Location: *Boatswain's Point*
Depth: *20-60ft (6-18m)*
Access: *Shore or boat*
Range: *Intermediate*

Only 20 minutes north of town, this site makes a pleasant getaway from Seven Mile Beach. Being a popular shore and night dive, many divers do this site by land, but it can also be dived by boat. There are two main attractions here: a mini-wall and a tarpon cave.

DiveTech@Turtle Reef is a dive facility located on the northwest tip of Grand Cayman. Part of a complex that includes the Cracked Conch restaurant and bar, it's a short walk from the newly renovated turtle farm facility. There is a good outdoor bar and eating area right on the sea; divers actually walk right by the bar to reach a ladder. Tanks can be rented here as well as all dive gear. If you're all dived out and just want to watch other divers and the water, grab a table or a barstool.

Head down the ladder in the protected channel that leads out to this dive. It's normally calm, but if there is a swell, time your entry so the wave pulls you out into the middle of the channel where you can put on your fins.

A roughly 50 yard swim over a flat reeftop leads to a vertical mini-wall that runs from 25ft to 60ft. Elephant ear, tube and vase sponges adorn the wall, as well as gorgonian fans and curious gray and queen angels. The sandy area below has both southern rays and patterned little lemon rays, while eagle rays are often reported here too. To get to the tarpon cave, take a right and swim along the wall until you reach the obvious cave area on the left. It's about a five-minute swim from the buoy marking the drop-off area.

There are a number of coral islands of various sizes off the wall in sand at 50ft to 60ft. Along with lots of fish in the mini-islands and nice coral cover, you may also find hawksbill sea turtles.

The cave holds the biggest thrill here, where 40 to 50 tarpon can usually be seen in the cave. Approach this cave slowly at about 45ft and they should remain in place. The cave isn't especially deep or dark, so one can enter a little way and watch the school of 3ft to 6ft long silvery fish for quite a while. When finished, have a look at the coral islands on your way back to the cut.

It is best not to go deeper here, as there is a plain further down where currents can kick up and create problems. Do the deeper reaches as a boat dive either at **Northwest Point** or **Dolphin Point.**

It is normally easy to get out of cut via the ladder, but as with entry, you'll need to time your exit in order to grab the ladder and step up quickly if there is a strong swell.

Tarpon file out from the cave at Turtle Farm

12 NORTHWEST POINT

Location: *West Bay*
Depth: *70-130ft (18-30m)*
Access: *Boat*
Range: *Intermediate*

This is a deep site at the far end of West Bay. Depending on the wind and waves, this dive isn't always possible, as being at the far tip of Grand Cayman, currents can be strong at times. This is good, however, for attracting sea life.

Head down the mooring line to the 60ft to 70ft range, then head out to the wall. There are some well-adorned spur and grooves here with marine growth that includes a couple of immense star coral heads, orange elephant ear sponges, some nice brain corals and large purple-tip sea anemones.

Fish life can include eagle rays and even Caribbean reef sharks out in the blue. Look also for resting nurse sharks and roaming green sea turtles. There are many cleaning stations along the wall and up on the grooves. Other fish to watch for include small blennies (including the beautiful diamond blenny) and some big honeycomb cowfish.

Keep in mind how deep the start of this dive is and watch the currents. Your air can go quickly at these depths, so give yourself plenty of time and air to get to the mooring and ascend.

Creole wrasse feed at the drop-off

13   BONNIE'S ARCH

Location: *South of Northwest Point*
Depth: *30-80ft (9-22m)*
Access: *Boat*
Range: *Intermediate*

Named after popular Cayman photographer Bonnie Charles, this is a great site that should be dived at the 80ft and above region, as the current-swept plain below can make things uncomfortable. There is so much to see here that a diver needs to only go about 60ft or so to take in a lot. Features to see include an arch, a partial cavern and a mini-wall leading to the sandy valley at 70ft to 80ft.

This site is best suited for smaller groups, as the more interesting features here are easily stirred up by bubbles and too many fins. A good site for macro and fish photos, wide angle folk may find that once they've shot the arch there's not much in the way of other features that are particularly appropriate for their lenses.

Most divers head first to the arch for a look. A well-adorned natural structure with some sponge and coral growth on top and hanging in the window, the arch itself is rather narrow and divers should watch their breathing so as not to scour the marine life with rising bubbles.

The arch is usually a magnet for horse-eye jacks and tarpon, which hang at about 60ft to 65ft inside the open cavern and can make for some pretty shots in here, if the light's right. Look around for smaller juveniles too. To the right of the mooring over along a mini-wall there's also a small cavern at about 50ft to 60ft. This is a very good place to see macro creatures like arrow crabs, brittle stars and neon gobies, as well as black coral. The silt is very fine, however, so shoot fast then get out, as bubbles hit the top of this indent and rain down fine silt.

Go to Hell

The jagged limestone rock formations in Grand Cayman's northwest once inspired a local official to exclaim, 'This is what Hell must look like.' Since then, the local post office has been painted fire-engine red and contains a resident 'devil' who asks 'How the hell are you?' as he dispenses souvenirs. He's quite a character, who likes to pose with pretty women and even has postcards of himself at **Stingray City** for sale.

But most visitors come here not so much for a free gander at the rugged limestone fields out in back of the facility, but to mail a card or letter from inside the gift shop so it has the postal mark from Hell. It's not every day your friends back home get a message from Hell. Or if you prefer, you can also bring them a T-shirt from Hell, or take a photo of one of the road signs on the island roads pointing to Hell.

A great variety of juveniles can be seen here, including baby queen angels, soapfish and flamingo tongues. Look too for rock beauties, lobsters walking about the reef, lots of small coral heads and other growth like sea plumes and gorgonian fans. There is usually a large great barracuda or two around here as well.

Juvenile queen angelfish

14 ORANGE CANYON

Location: *South of Northwest Point*
Depth: *50-130ft (18-40m)*
Access: *Boat*
Range: *Intermediate*

Although a deep dive, this is a popular site thanks to the colorful beauty of the huge elephant ear sponges to be found on this healthy and active reef.

Head down the mooring line and then out to the wall, which becomes apparent at around 100ft where it drops off into the blue. The deep grooves that lead out to the wall have varied sponge growth, including nice rope and barrel sponge growth – it's along these groove faces that the big elephant ears also grow. Fish life is also very good with lots of blue chromis, Creole wrasse schools, turtles and eagle rays.

The site is full of deep crevices and many swim-throughs. One particularly scenic spot is a round spire of rock with lots of fish to see. One of photo pro Cathy Church's favorites, this popular and fun site has lots going on both deep and at the top around the mooring.

15 SENTINEL ROCK

Location: *South of Northwest Point*
Depth: *70-130ft (22-40m)*
Access: *Boat*
Range: *Intermediate*

Located near **Orange Canyon**, this is a deep site that shares some of the same characteristics, such as good sponge life and a small pinnacle that attracts an interesting mix of marine life.

The mooring is secured in 70ft of water. There can be currents at this site, so it's best to exercise caution here or follow your guide, who can take a route that may offer some protection. There are some good swim-throughs here, as well as big rope sponges, sea plumes and purple-tipped sea anemones.

Look for green sea turtles, yellow jacks and silvery bar jacks, lots of black durgons and Creole wrasse, as well as dog snappers moving through the water around the pinnacle and above the wall. A large great barracuda likes to hang in the canyon near the mooring.

As this dive starts at 70ft, be sure to watch your air and time.

Active deep drop-off attracts fish and sea turtles

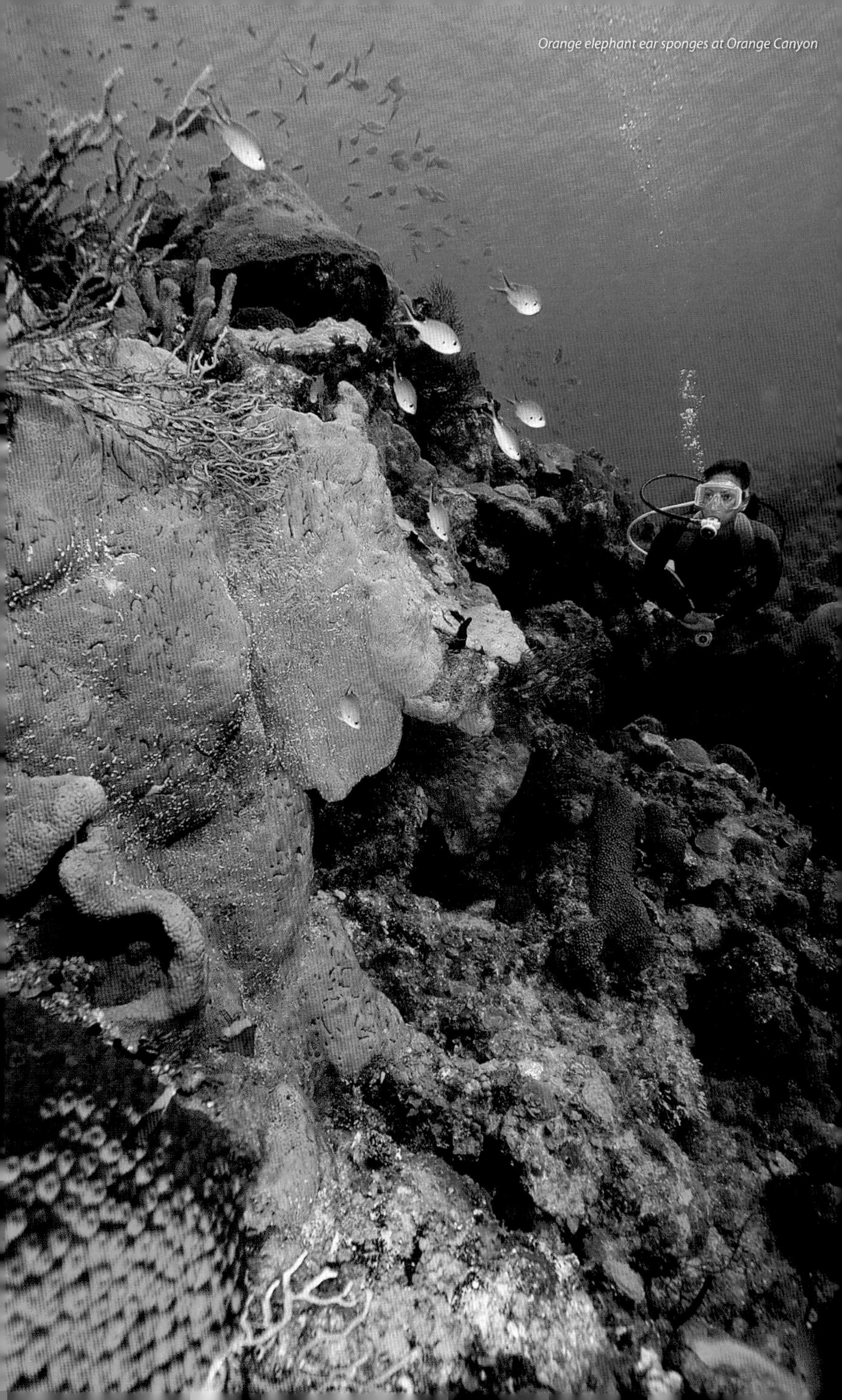

Orange elephant ear sponges at Orange Canyon

About Shore Diving

Seven Mile Beach

Several factors combine to offer Cayman Islands visitors some excellent shore diving opportunities. There are a number of easily accessible marked entry points to choose from, the Grand Caymans' normally calm west coast waters make entering the water safe and easy, and with a reef or drop-off no more than 50 yards offshore, surface swims are kept to a minimum.

Often you can just dip in at the entry point and swim out whilst enjoying the scenery, as the reeftop will have small sea fans and herbivorous fish pecking around. Freedom-loving divers are sure to enjoy the unlimited shore diving packages some dive centers offer.

Note that while auto break-ins are not common here, they can happen, so it's best to not leave valuables in the car, especially not in plain sight.

16 | BIG TUNNEL

Location: *Southeast of Northwest Point*
Depth: *55-100ft (17-30m)*
Access: *Boat*
Range: *Intermediate*

This site is known for its maze-like features, along with the big tunnel to swim through which provided its name. This honeycomb of a dive starts at 55ft and if this is a new dive site, you should follow a guide, as the many holes in this maze are best left to someone experienced to help you negotiate. Head down through canyons to the wall face – the tunnel mouth is at about 100ft and is perhaps 35ft wide. There may be silversides inside in season and it's also home to silver tarpon.

The wall is very good as well, with sea anemones, bright orange elephant ear sponges, brown and yellow tube sponges, rope sponges, large barrel sponges and black coral trees. Horse-eye and yellow jacks are commonly seen in the area and this is also a good spot to see eagle rays.

Up top around the mooring, there is nice hard coral here French and queen angelfish, cruising bar jacks and grunts around the sparse sea plumes, and other soft corals up shallow. You may also encounter southern stingrays in the sand.

Tube sponges

A diamond blenny peers out from a sea anemone

Divers emerge beneath a canopy of plate coral patrolled by Spanish hogfish, coneys and stoplight parrotfish. A nearby pinnacle also has a lot of marine life, and the reef slope is thick with deepwater gorgonians, huge masses of orange elephant ear sponges and drum-sized barrel sponges, some six feet in diameter.

A large variety of fish are seen here, including the beautiful scrawled filefish, queen and rock beauty angels, endless processions of Creole wrasse being cleaned and moving along the reef and, if you're lucky, an eagle ray. Keep an eye out in the blue for turtles and other blue water critters. Up in the shallows, sea plumes hide trumpetfish.

18 ROUND ROCK

Location: *Northern West Bay*
Depth: *60-80ft (18-24m)*
Access: *Boat*
Range: *Intermediate*

The two moorings here lead right down to rich reef life. Designated Round Rock East and West, in-between these two is a large, broad pinnacle, cut with swim-throughs that are easy to navigate. The reeftop has finger corals, sea anemones and lots of small fish life, including colorful juveniles and blue chromis.

Round Rock is a nicely landscaped site that is very good for wide angle photos as there are many spots here with beautiful overlapping plate corals. Numerous elephant ear sponges and other encrusting and tube sponges are to be found along the wall, which is covered in sea plumes, black coral trees and rope sponges.

Divers often check one particular large elephant's ear sponge to see how it is doing, as it was once broken but still manages to thrive.

17 LITTLE TUNNELS

Location: *Northwest West Bay*
Depth: *60-100ft (18-30m)*
Access: *Boat*
Range: *Intermediate*

Another site where the honeycomb of this coast becomes a fun sport dive, there is a swim-through about 70ft away from the base of the mooring. Follow your guide from the field of garden eels at the sandy flats 65ft down to the outer wall at approximately 85ft.

Don't Touch the Coral

Wonder why touching the coral is such a big deal? Stony coral is the only animal in the world that can be injured or killed simply by being pressed against its own skeleton. Unlike the rounded bones of other animals, the skeleton of stony coral is razor sharp, and the slightest contact slices living coral against itself.

The coral animals that create a coral head are only a few cell layers thick. To visualize this, imagine a tissue draped over a razorblade, misted with water. Just as any contact would tear the tissue against the razorblade, in the same way contact with stony corals pushes coral tissue against its own razor-sharp skeleton.

To avoid coral damage, divers are asked to not wear gloves in the Caymans.

19 | TRINITY CAVES

Location: *Northern West Bay*
Depth: *60-80ft (18-24m)*
Access: *Boat*
Range: *Intermediate*

These open caverns are very popular, being well-lit and full of life. Actually very deep and somewhat tight canyons starting at about 60ft, they drop down to the wall's edge at 100ft. Hard corals are abundant and schooling fish can be found in the protected areas.

The east canyon has a stunning arch that makes a good prop for wide angle photography, while the drop-off has an outcrop-type pinnacle with quivering deepwater gorgonians, large black coral growths and Creole wrasse all around. The pinnacle also holds very good sponge growth, with massive barrel sponges and some nice basket sponges dominating the topography.

Returning upwards again, follow one of the 'caves' back up to the shallow part of the reef, where sea whips and plumes hold cover for groupers and trumpetfish.

20 | SAND CHUTE

Location: *Northern West Bay*
Depth: *70-100ft (9-15m)*
Access: *Boat*
Range: *Intermediate*

One of the more striking deep dives along the wall, this is easier than those up at the northwest part of West Bay, as currents are not normally strong here.

An extremely broad sand plain here spills down through the wall. So broad it appears to be the width of a football field, it makes a veritable palace for the garden eels which have taken up residence. Hogfish can also be seen picking through the sand.

The edges of the spillway have good sponge life and black coral in some spots. This is all in the 70ft to 80ft range area and deeper, with many overhangs and pockets in the reef that provide good habitat.

Your guide may decide to get back to the mooring by taking a coral tunnel back up the 35-degree slope. Look for sleeping turtles here and check the cleaning stations for action.

Filefish hide in soft corals

Fairy basslets flit around a coral head

21 DOC POLSON WRECK

Location: *West Bay*
Depth: *40-60ft (18-30m)*
Access: *Boat*
Range: *Intermediate*

This sunken tug is very good for both macro photography and wide angle images. Stripped of almost anything that could hang up a diver, penetration is simple, as there are many openings and there is always a lot of light.

Depending on who's been there before you, the first thing that may greet you is a toilet. Perhaps this feature blew into the area from Hurricane Ivan, but in any case it's certainly not a ship's head. Often moved around, it can be found at various places on the ship, but if someone has put it on top of the bridge (wheelhouse), it will be the first thing you see when descending.

Since it has been cut and cleared for penetration, carefully swim inside and try not to stir up too much silt. Fin lightly, be neutrally buoyant and move with small movements. Inside there are many good macro subjects, including lettuce leaf nudibranchs, barber pole shrimp sitting in sponges, corkscrew anemones and mantis shrimp.

Underwater Weddings

Tying the knot down under can be done on a private charter boat trip, shore dive or even a night dive. Dive shops and hotels are used to having not only brides and grooms but also entire wedding parties coming to dive, stay and have the reception, with many dive shops assisting in planning and having packages. Some divers have a land wedding plus an underwater ceremony. Consider inviting a few stingrays to your service – they won't drink much, but they'll wipe out the calamari!

Be careful, as there are still a few stray wires in the bow and aft hold, along with one in the bridge which could hang a diver up, though they are pretty big and avoidable. Some nice light shafts come into the aft of the ship, and while its upper surface isn't overly covered in coral, it does have some fans, sponges and sea plumes on it. Look for slender filefish in the sea plumes at the bow.

Outside of the ship fish, the not-so-common Nassau grouper can be seen here at times, along with French angels and yellowtail snapper. The reef across from the wreck is also not bad, and the sandy flat has garden eels, many juveniles and lots of roaming parrotfish.

A Nassau grouper uses the wreck for refuge

Lobsters like the West Bay reefs

also include large brain corals, gorgonian sea fans and scattered plate corals. Almost anything can pop up here, and scrawled filefish, eagle rays and southern stingrays are apt to be seen.

23 | AQUARIUM SOUTH & NORTH

Location: *West Bay*
Depth: *30-50ft (9-15m)*
Access: *Boat*
Range: *Novice*

22 | MITCH MILLER'S

Location: *West Bay*
Depth: *35-70ft (18-30m)*
Access: *Boat or shore*
Range: *Intermediate*

This site was named for a famous TV show pioneer who had the show *'Sing Along With Mitch'.* A highly popular show in its time, it afforded Mr Miller the luxury of a house in the Caymans, right on the beach by this site. While Mitch Miller's is sometimes shore dived, a boat is easier.

Shallow and sandy with many coral heads, gulleys, deep undercuts and a few small swim-throughs, the site has beautiful white sand and at 60ft to 70ft the plain spreads out with garden eels and scattered coral heads. The area around the reef drop-off is the best locale to explore. Lobsters hide under the overhangs and walk about the reef, and this is also a very good place to see corkscrew anemones and Pederson shrimp. Yellowhead jawfish can be seen bobbing up and down from their holes.

Schoolmasters, striped grunts, goatfish and other schooling fish circle the coral heads at 30ft to 40ft. The corals

The site has many corals, sponges and fish, including the ever-popular midnight parrotfish and queen angelfish. Being shallow, long dives can be made which allow you to enjoy all the marine life on offer.

Head down the mooring and you will probably be joined by some ubiquitous yellowtails. Sporadic coral growth in the form of purple sea fans, sea plumes and some star and brain corals can be found along all of the ridges and side walls with small undercuts and sandy grooves. Some yellow tube sponges and encrusting sponges thrive here as well.

This is a great incubation site and a good fish lens or macro set-up will garner good shots of tropical juveniles. Look for boxfish, cowfish, juvenile butterflyfish, adult four-eye butterflyfish, slender filefish, yellowtails, a school of soldierfish and some very curious mutton snapper that appear to be waiting for a handout. Marauding schools of blue tang sometimes come through looking for algae patches to devour – they make a colorful photo subject if you anticipate their movements and get close enough for a photo.

Such varied fish life here, along with the shallow and clear water, certainly make The Aquarium live up to its name.

Wreck Diving in the Caymans

The Caymans is a good place to get a wreck certification. The water is clear, most wrecks are small and open, and they're also not all that deep. While the islands have a history as a major place for ships to hit, the wrecks that many divers encounter in West Bay have been sunk with diving in mind. Having been cleared of wires and doors that can trap divers, they are considered pretty safe to explore. They are also magnets for marine life, with many unusual and colorful creatures to be found in and around them.

The engine room of the Oro Verde

24 PETER'S (GOVERNOR'S) REEF

Location: *West Bay*
Depth: *35-50ft (9-15m)*
Access: *Boat*
Range: *Novice*

Many divers enjoy this shallow dive daily. There are plenty of fish here, possibly partly due to the reef's namesake, dive operator Peter Milburn, who liked to feed the resident fish. Known for his conservation efforts, the reef is also close to the governor's beachside residence.

There is a mooring here in about 35ft and the terrain around it is similar to that of The Aquarium, with coral covered spurs and small coral heads, sponges and plenty of fish life.

The site is known for its angelfish with French, gray, queen and rock beauties all to be found. All are friendly, so Peter's Reef is also a very good site for photographers.

The reefs also hold big green morays, parrotfish and spotted rums (look under ledges for these). Great for long and leisurely dives, this place is ideal for getting plenty of fish portraits.

25 ORO VERDE

Location: *West Bay*
Depth: *25-60ft (7-18m)*
Access: *Boat*
Range: *Intermediate*

While this wreck is pretty much broken up due to storms over the years, its proximity to **Peter's Reef** in the shallows above it and the fact that it still provides a lot of habitat for fish and small creatures makes it an interesting dive site. Its depth is also attractive, allowing long dives to be made on the ship and reefs nearby.

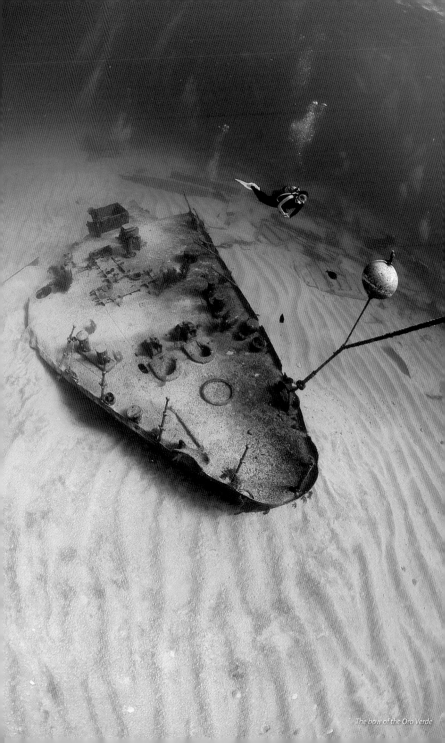

The bow of the Oro Verde

Dive boats and coral reef below the clear West Bay waters

Cayman dive pioneer Bob Soto sank the ship in 1980 to purposely create an artificial reef. Legend has it that it was a drug smuggler's ship and the name means 'Green Gold' in Spanish, so you can speculate as to what the cargo was. The ship was a little over 180ft in length, but the bow is now separated so it spans a much greater distance across the sandy plain. The bow still sits upright and has a mooring buoy on it, and there is usually little or no current at the site.

Don't be surprised if you're greeted by French angels on descent. While fish feeding isn't practiced all that much in the Caymans away from **Stingray City,** divemasters sometimes take a bit of fruit down, such as orange pulp, to entice fish in close to divers. The angels seem to like this and it seems pretty harmless. It certainly makes it great for photography.

The rest of the wreck also has a buoy leading down to it. As the sides have collapsed somewhat, it's easy to swim around and explore. Take care though, as some of the metal is jagged. The ship is not overly covered in growth on either section, but there's a little gorgonian on what appears to be the compass, and the engine room is splayed wide open, exposing the big machine.

The reef nearby has some nice macro critters, including yellowhead jawfish that have holes in the sand at about 50ft. Garden eels also live in the sandy 50ft to 60ft plain. Huge mutton snapper float about the wreck and there are also big tiger groupers here. Jacks, yellow coneys, lizardfish and scrawled cowfish all make good photo subjects.

This is also a good night dive – look for arrow crabs and wandering hermits.

26 | HAMMERHEAD HOLE

Location: *West Bay*
Depth: *30-50ft (9-15m)*
Access: *Boat*
Range: *Novice*

This is a shallow dive that can provide a lot of bottom time. It's not clear exactly how the hammerhead moniker came about, but nurse sharks seem fond of the site. Scalloped hammerheads do like to eat stingrays, so they are around Grand Cayman but they're not necessarily seen here with any regularity.

You're more likely to see French angels, parrotfish and snappers as you descend to the pin at 30ft. From there, coral spurs and sandy grooves hold various holes, undercuts and encrusting corals.

Approximately 10 to 12 minute's swim south out to a long coral spur, the fifth one from the mooring line, is an area that nurse sharks seem to like. If you are lucky, one will be resting under a ledge or near the reef in the sand. Eagle rays also like to hunt in the sand past the reef. Head out here first if you're into sharks, then make your way back up to the shallows.

Stoplight parrotfish

27 | CARIBBEAN SANDCHUTE

Location: *West Bay*
Depth: *50-130ft (16-40m)*
Access: *Boat*
Range: *Intermediate*

This is a beautiful site to see, with a broad sandy plain spilling out to a drop-off at 100ft. The mooring buoy sits in 45ft of water and the chute is quite obvious. Visibility and the reflective power of the sand combine to make this a site that allows you to see a long way.

At the drop-off, a small coral island attracts a lot of marine life, including a school of horse-eye jacks. The island also has a few large vase sponges and growths of plate and castle coral. Look too for black coral trees a bit deeper.

High ridges rising up to 45ft on either side of the chute have a lot of fish life – green eels and toothy great barracuda join schools of chromis and blue-striped grunts.

The chute itself is a pretty place to swim over at the 60ft to 70ft level. Beautiful waves have naturally formed in the sand and southern stingrays move silently, floating like alien hovercraft.

28 | RHAPSODY (MESA)

Location: *West Bay*
Depth: *30-60ft (9-18m)*
Access: *Boat*
Range: *Novice*

Rhapsody is a good dive for colorful angels and parrotfish in the shallower waters. Located along the same upper reef area south of **Oro Verde,** it is called a mesa due to its high, flat, tabletop coral formation.

Flamingo tongue cowries can be found at the base of gorgonian corals

Drop down to the mooring at 35ft and head for the reef sides which form a good mini-wall, adorned with hard corals, some sponge life and wire corals. The coral cover attracts blue-striped grunts, silver schoolmasters and snappers, while yellowtail also hang in the water column.

There are many cleaning stations. Look for coneys, tiger grouper and French and gray angelfish being cleaned or roaming the wall. Golden hamlets can also be found. Night diving is popular here, but there is some fire coral so be careful after dark and wear a skin suit for protection.

29 ROYAL PALMS LEDGE

Location: *West Bay*
Depth: *40-55ft (12-17m)*
Access: *Boat*
Range: *Novice*

The Royal Palms Hotel is no longer, but the ledge and its namesake site remain. The reef forms a horseshoe shape where divers can swim down to 40ft and start exploring.

This sandy u-shaped channel runs through the reef and is almost tunnel-like, being undercut quite deeply.

Sponge life here is good with big barrel sponges and tube sponges, while schooling horse-eye jacks and snapper are found around the channel. As you follow the channel, look for one particular spot where an undercut about 15ft high goes in quite deeply. Fish here swim upside-down, orienting themselves to the bottom.

Macro creatures include file shells, juvenile lobster, tunicate colonies and small shrimp. Royal Palms Ledge really shines at night with all this smaller life crawling around – keep an eye out for squid too.

30 CHEESEBURGER REEF

Location: *George Town Harbor*
Depth: *20-30ft (6-9m)*
Access: *Boat or shore*
Range: *Novice*

Also called Soto's Reef, this site is frequently used for intro dives, instruction and newer divers. Snorkelers are also taken here and it can get quite crowded with visitors from cruise ships late morning through into the afternoon.

The site has nice staghorn and elkhorn coral stands that attract schooling fish. Sitting right at the entrance to the harbor, the mooring is in only 12ft of water, but there are a lot of fish around here, with everything from schooling surgeonfish to big tarpon.

Keep an eye out for boat traffic. It's less crowded later in the day and on night dives.

A brain coral is the resting place for this peppermint blenny

Bring the Kids

For people travelling with kids, some dive shops will customize a package appropriate to the child's age, as well as the needs and experience of the individual. Some of the programs available are in-water programs by SSI Scuba Rangers/PADI Seal Team, Jr Open Water certifications and SASY Snorkeling.

Program	Age Range
SASY Snorkel Programs	5 and over
Scuba Rangers/Seal Team	8 and over
Jr Open Water Cert	10 and over

Check before you go to see if your dive operation is offering any or all of these programs. The clear water and calm inshore conditions, plus availability of pools at just about every locale, make the Caymans a good place to give youngsters proper ocean training and skills.

Even though nearby **Cheeseburger Reef** gets a lot of action, the *Balboa* isn't dived as heavily and marine life is very diverse. This is because permission must be given by the harbormaster, and in these times of tighter security, that can sometimes be a problem. Check with your dive shop about making this dive, as normally they can either call on the phone or by marine radio channel 16 to ask for permission. You don't need much notice, so this formality isn't as big a drawback as it might seem. If the harbormaster has a big cargo ship scheduled to enter the port, however, diving is likely to be restricted.

Saddled blenny

31 BALBOA

Location: *George Town Harbor*
Depth: *20-30ft (6-9m)*
Access: *Boat or shore*
Range: *Novice*

A freighter that was sunk in the 1930s following a hurricane, the *Balboa* is pretty much broken up now. However, the big props are still there and metal from the wreckage has spread out over a shallow area, creating habitat for a lot of different fish and invertebrates.

The ship was nearly 400ft long, and the debris area includes parts from the boiler room and stern. At night, orange ball coralimorphs (which look like orange tipped anemones) come out, and octopi, coneys and lizardfish also reside here.

32 EDEN ROCK & DEVIL'S GROTTO

Location: *South of George Town*
Depth: *20-40ft (6-12m)*
Access: *Shore*
Range: *Novice*

The limestone at Eden Rock is pocked with grottoes and caves, and there is plenty of fish as well. Entry can be made via the dive center located here, where you can ask about the layout of the reef. They'll not only show you a map but rent you a tank right then and there too.

This isn't a hard dive as there is usually no current and the fish are well fed, so snorkelers can enjoy the site as well. Since fish will approach closely, it's good for photographers too.

A hard reef flat and some corals and small fans make up a reef area high-

A tiny but colorful mantis shrimp

lighted by fish. Rock beauties, stoplight and red parrotfish, lots of sergeant majors, chubs and even tarpon can be seen.

Divers may find the caves interesting, especially if they are full of silversides and baitfish. Tarpon roam this pocked reef area as well, and the cracks and streaming light can make for good wide angle photos.

Seahorses

The seahorses found around the Cayman Islands aren't always that easy to see. They don't move much and normally aren't found on popular sites, instead living in the mangrove areas. Commonly called the longsnout seahorse, they can be brown, yellow, red and black with tiny dark spots evenly spread over the body. The snout is relatively long and they grow to be six inches tall, securing themselves to sea grasses or gorgonians with their tail to feed on plankton that drifts past.

While found throughout the Caribbean, this seahorse is rare north of Cuba. Divers and snorkelers seldom see them, however, because they mostly inhabit docks, pilings, floating mats of sea grass and other places people don't often explore. Check the dock at Rum Point or the sea grasses nearby – you might get lucky.

Continuing farther down the ironshore, Devil's Grotto can be reached in the same shallow dive and offers some of the same features, with little caves, grottoes and sunlit tunnels that have tarpon and schools of baitfish. Wide angle photos with interesting light patterns can be made in the cracks and caves.

33 | DON FOSTER'S REEF

Location: *South of George Town*
Depth: *12-50ft (4-16m)*
Access: *Boat or shore*
Range: *Novice*

Located at the southern edge of the West Wall, you can shore dive at Don Foster's and observe its sand flats with intermittent coral fingers leading down to the wall.

Don Foster's is located at Casuarina Point, which is also a good snorkeling and shallow dive area. Entry from the cement pier incorporated into the ironshore is easy. Do a giant stride in and then swim out along the protected finger to the upper reef area. There are offshore mooring buoys to swim to and go down if you want to save air.

Used by many as a check-out dive spot to get used to equipment again after a layoff from diving, the reef is part of the Cayman's Marine Park and is just an extension past the Devil's Grotto site, but with different terrain. It's an easy dive with easy access where you can see eels, turtles, lobster and scorpion fish, and if you make it to the big wall, there is great coral and sponge life. This can be a long swim, however, so it may be best to do the actual wall dive by boat.

Foster's has very good macro photography offerings as octopi and juveniles live here, so take the time to look around the coral growths atop the spurs and at the undercuts.

34 PARROT'S REEF

Location: *South of George Town*
Depth: *20-50ft (6-16m)*
Access: *Boat*
Range: *Novice*

Found about 90ft off the dock at Parrot's Landing, snorkeling and diving can both be done at this shallow site. Just swim out past the volcanic rock ironshore and start looking for critters.

The site has good growths of star and brain corals, while angelfish, snapper, French grunts and plenty of other fish find the reef appealing. Barrel and tube sponges are also part of the terrain, even though it is a fairly shallow dive. Look also for octopi here.

As the name implies, parrotfish often feed here and stoplight, queen and redband parrotfish are all to be seen. They like to feed upon the algae on the coral rocks. Consider making a night dive here to look for roaming octopi and parrotfish sleeping in their protective mucous domes within the reef's cracks.

35 SUNSET REEF & LCM DAVID NICHOLSON

Location: *South Sound*
Depth: *30-60ft (9-18m)*
Access: *Boat or shore*
Range: *Novice*

This site is the house reef for Sunset House hotel, with a small fee to dive here and use their pier facilities. Tanks and weight can be rented right at the dive window near the pier. Entry is easy and there are a couple of good photo opportunities at the site, including the statue of the Mermaid Amphitrite and

Queen Conchs

These large snails are afforded total protection in all three of the marine parks, as well as partial protection through the marine conservation laws which restrict the catching of conchs. Traditionally, conchs have formed an important part of the Cayman cultural cuisine, but increased human populations and the relative ease with which these creatures can be caught has depressed their numbers considerably all over the Caribbean.

Marine parks around the islands support a large population which is responsible for restocking the open areas, both through migration out of the park and the supply of larval conch which are dispersed by the ocean's currents.

Seagrass forms a vital role in the early stages of the conchs' life cycle. Snorkelers may also see young conch in mangrove and seagrass areas.

the shipwreck LCM *David Nicholson*. Both can be visited in the same dive.

As noted, shore entry is easy with a couple of places on the pier for a high giant stride or a water level giant stride. Once in, swim out along the sandy grooves looking for lettuce leaf nudibranchs and scorpionfish that may be in the area. You will soon see a nice reef area running from about 30ft to 55ft with some spurs and grooves. The reef has large brain corals, yellow tube sponges, sea plumes and many small hard corals. This is real macro country too, with Christmas tree worms, mantis shrimp, flamingo tongues, bristleworms and many other tiny creatures.

This is also a great night and dusk dive, so come here before sunset to watch the hamlets do their mating rituals. Once they start circling one another they don't seem to care if the camera is flashing away – shameless!

The wreck sits near the outer drop-off

Barrel Sponges

Barrel sponges in the Caymans can reach a diameter of more than six feet around and six feet high, providing habitat for cleaning shrimps and other small reef creatures. With a lifespan of over 100 years, sponges feed by pumping water in and out, gleaning nutrients from it in the process. Be very careful when diving near barrel sponges, as their rims are quite brittle and can break off easily, despite their size. This can seriously inhibit the sponge's ability to filter. Suppress the urge to climb inside to show how big a sponge is, as this is an easy way to damage one – pose beside it to give some size perspective.

Most barrel sponges are found in deeper water below the 50ft mark.

On the right side of the reef you can see the statue of the mermaid in the distance. Amphitrite has been overseeing Sunset Reef for several years now, and has graced the covers of *Skin Diver Magazine, Sport Diver Magazine, Scuba Diving Magazine* and numerous others. The creation of Canadian sculptor Simon Morris, she is a nine foot tall bronze mermaid, well anchored in 55ft of water. This statue makes for great wide angle photos, with yellowtails and French angelfish coming around to pose as auxiliary models.

Heading straight there, the swim to the mermaid from the entry takes roughly ten minutes. If you plan on diving both the mermaid and the shipwreck in the same dive, this is a good start as the wreck is another five minutes swim further out from the mermaid. Looking from the beach, it is the farthest buoy straight out from the entry. From the mermaid you'll have to angle across the sand a bit, but it is normally easy to see in the distance if conditions are calm.

The *Nicholson* is a former US WWII landing craft with some fish life and good purple tube sponges on it. It's not too grown over with marine life and makes a good wide angle photo prop, as does the mermaid.

The ship sits at the start of the deep wall (which is probably better done as a boat dive) and it should be your turning point for a pleasant shallow recreational dive. Swim back up to the reef and enjoy the fish life and occasional sea turtle that comes in here. Exit is easy with a long ladder, though if you have a camera you may have to hand it up to someone. There is usually little surge here, but if there is, time your exit to get on the ladder safely.

36 EAGLE RAY ROCK

Location: *North of Southwest Point*
Depth: *50-100ft (16-30m)*
Access: *Boat*
Range: *Intermediate*

The mooring here is in a little over 50ft and marks out a deeper dive with a big sand chute and some good coral spurs. Near the southern tip, this site isn't dived as much as some of the calmer inner bay sites. This can be good, as there seems to be a decent amount of fish life and eagle rays (which gave the site its name).

Head down the anchor line to the reeftop and the chute will become apparent. This has garden eels in residence, and there may also be southern stingrays hunting or covered in sand.

Head down through the groove to the canyon, which has healthy corals and some beautiful tube sponges.

This continues on the reef wall, which is beautifully adorned with barrel, rope and bright red encrusting sponges. Look too for black corals in well-formed trees.

Fish here include blue parrotfish, gray angels, blue chromis and an occasional moray eel.

A hawksbill sea turtle roams the reef

A diver examines a young flamingo tongue cowrie

South Sound

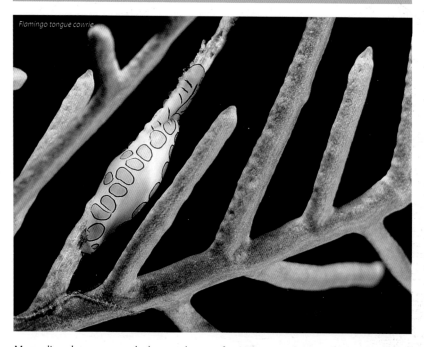
Flamingo tongue cowrie

Many dives here are much deeper than those in the nearby West Bay, and are also subject to surge conditions. However there is a good chance of seeing pelagic fish here and some sites have some very interesting topography.

37 JAPANESE GARDENS

Location: *South Sound*
Depth: *30-55ft (9-17m)*
Access: *Boat*
Range: *Intermediate*

Shallow and full of swim-throughs, this fun little dive allows lots of time to play around and discover.

Sand chutes at Japanese Gardens lead to various cuts and caverns. Look for tarpon and silversides (in season) in the caverns. Big barracuda also lurk here.

Hurricane waves have damaged the staghorn and elkhorn corals that gave the site its name, which is said to resemble a neat bonsai garden, but these are now rebounding.

Mar jacks, groupers, eagle rays and nurse sharks are all seen at this dive. Surge can be an issue here so it isn't dived a lot, but when the waves are flat it can be a very good dive.

South Sound	GOOD SNORKELING	NOVICE	INTERMEDIATE	ADVANCED
37 JAPANESE GARDENS		•	•	
38 CHRISTINA REEF & WALL		•	•	

Queen Elizabeth II Botanic Park

Grand Cayman's botanic park (☎ 345 947 3558; open 9am-6:30pm daily) is hard to beat and is the best place to experience the island's indigenous fauna in one compact area. The park is laid out with nature in mind, with well-marked trails winding through lush terrain. The walk is easy and takes you to open pens containing the rare blue iguana. These blend into the grasses well, but can be seen hanging from tree branches or sunning themselves on hills. Some also roam wild.

The woods have about 300 native plant species. Bring some insect repellant for when you walk past buttonwood swamps, mahogany forests and native palms – it can come in handy.

There is an attractive waterfowl pond which also holds some turtles, and a floral garden with many orchids (these bloom late May through June) and tropical plants and flowers. This is a great place for nature buffs and a nice drive along the south coast to reach it. The park also has a small gift shop.

38 | CHRISTINA REEF & WALL

Location: *South Sound*
Depth: *65-130ft (19-40m)*
Access: *Boat*
Range: *Intermediate*

One of the deepest on this side, this site has some very nice features. The mooring pin is in 65ft of water, so this will be a fairly short dive.

However, it can be a lot of fun as the deep spur and groove formations below the moorings lead to caverns and swim-throughs. These have attractive sponge life, including some brown tube sponges and rope sponges. Lots of small chromis and basslets gather around the bigger sponges.

Keep an eye out for hawksbill turtles and eagle rays in the blue, as well as dogtooth tuna and Caribbean reef sharks.

Remember to watch your time and air and head up with 700 pounds of air in your tank at the very least.

Schoolmasters like the upper reef

Divers encounter a barracuda

East Side & East End

Colorful new condos are popping up along the south east coast

Many of the sites here are among the most famous in the Caymans. Located far from major towns, this area has a laid-back atmosphere. There is a lot of shipwreck history here as well –much of it memorialized at small parks along the side of the road. Development is now coming to the area and condos, a major grocery store and some very nice restaurants can be found.

The diving offers rich marine life on walls full of crevices and swim-throughs, along with a good chance of seeing pelagic marine life.

East Side and East End sites are not usually as crowded with boats and divers as other areas, so chances are good that if you want to visit a given site you will be able to.

East Side & East End Site	GOOD SNORKELING	NOVICE	INTERMEDIATE	ADVANCED
39 CRUSHER'S WALL			•	•
40 BIG HOUSE WALL			•	•
41 IRONSHORE GARDENS			•	•
42 PLAYING FIELD		•	•	
43 SHARK ALLEY		•	•	
44 THE MAZE			•	•
45 MCKENNEY'S CANYON			•	•
46 PAT'S WALL			•	•
47 SCUBA BOWL			•	•
48 GROUPER GROTTO		•	•	
49 SNAPPER HOLE		•	•	
50 VALLEY OF THE DOLLS		•	•	
51 BABYLON			•	•

Beautiful tube sponges at Big House Wall

also be seen quivering in the current here, surrounded by blue chromis. Look too for a few purple gorgonian sea fans, finger sponges, star corals and hovering sergeant majors, along with a large branching anemone nestled in the hard corals on the reef.

Heading back, there is a deep swim-through canyon lined with purple sea fans, which takes you back up to the reef. There are some large sea fans here, while fish include marauding jacks, a number of great barracuda and some colorful bicolor damsels.

Make your way back to the anchor line and do your safety stop, as this is a pretty but quite deep dive.

40 | BIG HOUSE WALL

Location: *Southeast of Half Moon Bay*
Depth: *65-130ft (9-15m)*
Access: *Boat*
Range: *Intermediate*

Local dive shops are referring to an actual big house (not the federal jail) on the shore line when naming this site. This reef has a deep mooring, so head down the line where you will see a large coral-covered groove with sand channels on both sides, along with a wall covered in big, yellow tube sponges and a good swim-through.

On the reef look for large sea plumes which sometimes hide a trumpetfish or two. Large brain corals are accented by purple gorgonian sea fans, while long, erect rope sponges grow here too.

Keep an eye out for hawksbill sea turtles on the reef, along with spiny lobsters hiding in nooks and crannies. Another deep dive with extremely clear water, it pays to keep an eye on your depth gauge and air supply here. Closer to shore, Big House Wall is also a good dive with shallow caverns.

39 | CRUSHER'S WALL

Location: *Southeast of Half Moon Bay*
Depth: *65-130ft (9-15m)*
Access: *Boat*
Range: *Intermediate*

For this dive, local dive shops actually drop an anchor in a large sand chute. Head down the line and then over to the wall. There is a beautiful outcrop just over the wall loaded with attractive marine life.

Look for bright red rope sponges on the outcrop. Deepwater gorgonians can

41 | IRONSHORE GARDENS

Location: *Southeast of Half Moon Bay*
Depth: *30-55ft (9-15m)*
Access: *Boat*
Range: *Intermediate*

The limestone coastline is referred to as the ironshore, and this interesting and shallow site is a favorite for those looking for tarpon and small fish. There is a mini-wall covered in hard corals and purple gorgonian sea fans, along with an exciting area of winding tunnels and caves.

This maze is where divers go to photograph and observe tarpon and small schools of horse eye jacks. One particular cavern is home to a rare (for the Caymans) school of glassy sweepers. Smaller fish include four-eye butterflyfish, juvenile French angels and schoolmasters in the shallows around the elkhorn corals.

In the dive briefing, your guide will show you a cavern called the Ear Hole, west of the mooring. To dive this ear canal-like swim-through, follow your guide, as it is fun but somewhat hard to find.

42 | PLAYING FIELD

Location: *Southeast of Half Lower Bay*
Depth: *30-50ft (9-15m)*
Access: *Boat*
Range: *Novice*

The top area of this interesting little patch reef has been somewhat hurricane scoured, so the beautiful elkhorns are not what they once were, though they still attract schools of grunts, schoolmasters and snappers.

A series of spurs feature sea fans aplenty up top and undercut areas below. Look for decorator crabs on the flowing purple gorgonians, which sometimes look just like a piece of brown algae.

Spotted scorpionfish, longspine squirrelfish, beautiful juvenile spotted rums with flowing fins and triplefins are all seen here. One extremely cute little guy is the spinyhead blenny, which occupies a hole in the coral and makes various faces from his home. This fishy spot also has French angelfish, four-eye butterflyfish, chubs and Creole wrasse schools.

A spinyhead blenny

Caribbean reef shark with a fish hook
photo: J. Dietz

43 SHARK ALLEY

Location: *South Sound*
Depth: *40-65ft (13-21m)*
Access: *Boat*
Range: *Novice*

This site first came about when progressive dive shop Ocean Frontiers wanted to start a shark education program and a shark feed to go with it. The program once entailed an hour and a half of education and presentations before the dive, and then a half-hour debrief afterward. However, the whole experience had to be dropped, as Cayman law states 'no one may feed, attempt to feed or provide or use food to attract any shark in Cayman waters'. (Never mind that the stingrays fed elsewhere are members of the shark family.)

The good news is that sharks don't easily forget where they get a free meal, so while you'd be extra-lucky if 10 sharks showed up at a time, as they once did, divers can now usually expect to see a Caribbean reef shark or two heading back in from the blue at the sound of their boat's arrival. Sit still on the bottom and don't chase the sharks; they may get close enough to see and if you're very lucky, close enough for a photo.

If the sharks don't show, look out for lobsters, angelfish and spotted drums on the reef. There is no buoy here; just an anchor drop in the sand.

A diver and yellowtail snapper examine a large brain coral

44 THE MAZE

Location: *Southeast of East Point*
Depth: *40-100ft (12-30m)*
Access: *Boat*
Range: *Intermediate*

This dive is pretty much as its name promises, and starts in about 40ft with the wall topping out at around 65ft. This is the beginning point for a playground of passages, swim-throughs and steep, plate-coral adorned canyon walls that soar like the side of the Grand Canyon.

The wall is just outside the South Channel, making it a good location for spotting pelagic fish, so look out for Caribbean reef sharks, blacktips and even a bull shark or rare manta ray. A pretty well-known large green sea turtle also lives in the area.

Whilst keeping an eye on the blue, don't neglect the main wall, with its outcrop pinnacle adorned in plate and brain corals, rope sponges and dancing chromis.

When finishing this exciting dive, head back up via one of the many canyonways.

45 MCKENNEY'S CANYON

Location: *Southeast of East Point*
Depth: *60130ft (18-40m)*
Access: *Boat*
Range: *Intermediate*

This was once the favorite haunt of the late underwater filmmaker Jack McKenney, who brought us diving dogs and his own style of abalone iron. Vertical canyons lead to the deepest drop-off in the northern hemisphere, which plunges 25,000ft down, down, down… Some

say it is also the East End's number one dive site for sharks and eagle rays.

The dive starts deep with the wall crest by the mooring pin at 70ft, with beautiful canyonlike terrain sliced with tunnels and overgrown swim-throughs. Some immense purple gorgonian sea fans are found here, along with giant yellow and brown tube sponges. Normally seen at shallower depths, flamingo tongues like the bases of gorgonians down here.

Being on the island's southeastern-most point, look for pelagic life, including dogtooth tuna, Caribbean reef sharks and blacktips out in the blue.

Remember just how deep this dive starts, as the water here is normally very clear so it's easy to lose track of depth. When heading up, make sure you have at least 700 pounds and more than 50 bar for your ascent and deco stop.

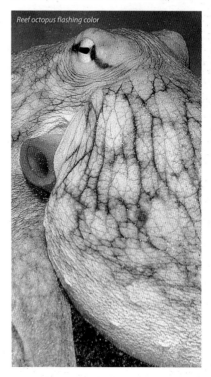
Reef octopus flashing color

46 | PAT'S WALL

Location: *Southeast of East Point*
Depth: *60-100ft (18-30m)*
Access: *Boat*
Range: *Intermediate*

This site was named in honor of Patricia Shar, a manager of the Cayman Diving Lodge in the 1980s. One of the most exposed areas of the East End wall, it is also as exciting as most of the dives here, with an intricate series of passageways to explore. Be sure to watch the briefing and follow the guide through the terrain, if its your first dive here.

Big, bushy sea plumes in this canyon country hide trumpetfish and tiger groupers. Deepwater sea fans are abundant and healthy, as are lush black coral trees and sponge communities of yellow and brown tubes.

The largest schools of fish hang out right by the mooring pin on a very pronounced buttress of coral. The wall plummets straight down between 100ft and 150ft, and then down to 6,000ft and more – wild country. Enjoy this site, but manage your time and depth well. As it's quite an exposed location, take care when getting into the boat, as seas can kick up at any time.

Huge whip corals are at Pat's

47 | SCUBA BOWL

Location: *Southeast of East Point*
Depth: *70-100ft (22-30m)*
Access: *Boat*
Range: *Intermediate*

Once described as a structural slalom course, this deep plunge winds divers in and out of a craggy coral wall and out to the main drop-off. Here, two large pinnacles and a massive mushroom formation resembling a church spire can be explored.

Deepwater gorgonians found here are among the largest in the Caymans.

Wreck of the Ten Sails Park

Part of the craggy coastline at the eastern tip of Grand Cayman, this park commemorates the island's most legendary shipwreck. On a fateful night in February 1794, the *Cordelia,* leading a convoy of merchant ships bound from Jamaica to Britain, ran aground on the reef at East End.

In a tragic case of crossed signals, the warning issued from the *Cordelia* to the other ships was misinterpreted as a call to follow more closely, and so one by one another nine ships crashed into the reef.

Fortunately for the imperiled sailors, the able mariners living on the island's craggy East End sprang into action, showing great heroism in ensuring that no lives were lost. Popular legend states that as a reward, King George III granted the islands eternal freedom from taxation. Even though actual records do not entirely support this story, the tale seems permanently ingrained in Caymanian lore (and possibly served as an inspiration for the contemporary tax code).

Scorpionfish are masters of camouflage

48 GROUPER GROTTO

Location: *Southeast of East Point*
Depth: *25-50ft (8-15m)*
Access: *Boat*
Range: *Novice*

This is a good site for macro and fish photography. Grouper Grotto is located just to the east of the South Channel and could be described as a classic Cayman East End reef. It has a tabletop and corals coming up to within 20ft of the surface, and sea fans, sea whips, elkhorn corals and big brain corals all adorn the reef.

A honeycombed reef of canyons, chutes and archways, this place is teeming with fish. Look for such usual suspects as the Nassau, black and tiger groupers, great barracuda and yellowtail snapper.

There are silversides here, and tarpon can usually be found too. The tarpon school here can be quite large depending on the time of year. If you are lucky, you may get to watch them working together to drive the baitfish into a tight ball before darting in for a meal. A squadron of eagle rays resides here as well, when there is some current running along the outer reef.

Grouper Spawn

Groupers usually live an isolated existence around the Cayman Islands. However, after the first full moon in January, and for about a month after that, they gather at specific reef locations to form huge spawning aggregations.

Line fishing for groupers at the spawning sites around all three islands is restricted to persons normally resident on the islands.

Black coral, star coral and tube sponges also thrive amid dancing schools of Creole wrasse and blue chromis. Reef sharks often patrol the blue water.

The area dive shop, Ocean Frontiers, sometimes make a great drift dive here; as it is so deep, a little more time can be spent enjoying the terrain. An open water deco is done before a boat pickup.

A banded coral shrimp

49	SNAPPER HOLE

Location: *East of Colliers Bay*
Depth: *35-65ft (11-20m)*
Access: *Boat*
Range: *Novice*

Yet another eastern classic, this site has long been a haunt of underwater photographers looking for a lot of bottom time in a scenic area.

A labyrinth of tunnels, cuts and coral-laden caverns filled with striped snappers, schoolmasters and tarpon hanging around for silversides (when they're in season), it is also a spawning area for some of the year.

Snapper Hole also features an 1872 Spanish anchor and a rare formation of pillar coral. For the macro shooter, there are lettuce leaf nudibranchs, flamingo tongues and roughead blennies.

50	VALLEY OF THE DOLLS

Location: *East of Colliers Bay*
Depth: *65-130ft (20-40m)*
Access: *Boat*
Range: *Novice*

Someone had a sense of humor when naming this beautiful and dreamy reef after the bestseller pulp fiction (and later major motion picture) by author Jacqueline Susanne.

A wide angle delight, healthy coral growth makes this an East End underwater studio. Highly photogenic, it features lots of props like barrel sponges, yellow tube sponges and an array of rope sponges entangled on the wall. Feather plume growth on the reeftop is very tall and broad, including an eight foot high growth that can dwarf a diver, found just north of the mooring pin.

The site's main navigation feature is a huge canyon that splits the main coral buttress and serves as a perfect entrance on to the wall. Fish life here is very good with big grouper and the occasional reef shark. A number of black coral species can be found here, with some very big coral trees.

51 BABYLON

Location: *North Shore, East of Old Man's Bay*
Depth: *55-100ft (17-30m)*
Access: *Boat*
Range: *Intermediate*

Offering a deep sea pinnacle and some very nice wall cover, this boat dive is one of the premium dives at this end of the island, and is considered one of Grand Cayman's best. It is becoming a regularly requested site from repeat divers. Ocean Frontiers runs a day-long three dive trip it calls the Three Tank Safari, which includes this dive along with whatever is available along the east and north sides of the island.

One of the finest walls in the Caymans, divers have reported a range of pelagic activity, including a large manta ray doing barrel roll feeding on plankton flowing off the reef.

There is a beautiful pinnacle off the wall, along with thick, diversified black coral growths and large deepwater gorgonians. Barrel sponges six foot around, multi-colored rope sponges and red encrusting sponges all make for a colorful dive. Schools of black durgon are thick in the water column and Creole wrasse make endless trains across the reeftop.

This dive isn't that deep, although if you swim over the wall crest at 50ft it can be a deep dive. There's a lot you can do at this Cayman highlight.

Spotted drum in transition

Silver Tarpon

There are some very good sites for viewing the large tarpon that like to school in valleys and open cave mouths along the Caymans' pocked terrain. Members of the *Megalops atlanticus* family, these creatures are famed as catch-and-release game fish, being strong fighters. When spawning the females release 13 million eggs.

Photographing these highly reflective fish can be a challenge. Choose a low strobe power setting and try to use it just as fill, while attempting to expose for both the fish and natural light around it. This should keep hard glare to a minimum and show the fish in its natural habitat. Alternately, expose just for the highly reflective fish and the background will likely go black or dark blue – this can be effective for portraits.

An iguana with plumeria in the background
photo: J. Dietz

The Sisters

Little Cayman beach

Just 90 miles northeast of Grand Cayman and serviced daily by air, the sister islands of Cayman Brac and Little Cayman are the epitome of Caribbean charm. Quiet and natural, both divers and nature-lovers like to make a point of spending a few days or a few weeks here as part of a Cayman visit. Some devoted Sisters fans simply come directly here for their entire holiday.

Cayman Brac is 14 miles long and two miles across at its widest. Noted for dramatic land topography, it has a majestic limestone bluff that forms a dragonback running west to east along the island's length. Ending at an overlook to Spot Bay on one end and Pollard Bay on the other, the ridge is pocked with natural caves and rough crevices. Some are said to be pirate caves from days gone by and tales of buried treasure still float around the bars after a few 'sundowners' loosen lips. The limestone also creates

some photogenic blowholes. Cayman Brac takes its name from the Gaelic word for bluff, and rock climbers have been increasingly eyeing these bluffs – and scaling a few. The road to the top of the bluff passes through the National Trust Parrot Reserve, the nesting ground for the islands' native green parrot species. Fruit trees, orchids, cacti and nice beaches highlight the island.

The majority of dives here, which includes a handful of shipwrecks, are done in the west end and the southwestern part of the island. But there are over 40 sites that can be dived depending on the weather, so you won't run out of choices relative to the small size of the place. There are also a number of dives on Little Cayman favored by Brac operators, so they make the bump across the channel on a pretty regular basis. If the sea is calm, this is fine, but it can be a pain in higher seas.

Little Cayman is smaller and much flatter but still rises to 56ft and is a mile wide. The majority of dives here are also done at the west end of the island, along both north and south shores. Little Cayman is famous for Bloody Bay Wall Marine Park, which features an extremely healthy and diverse Caribbean reef with walls starting in 20ft of water and plummeting to an abyss. Professional dive operations offer services ranging from day trips to instruction to underwater photography courses.

The nature theme continues inland with the 203-acre Booby Pond Nature Reserve, which is said to be a bird lover's dream and the nesting grounds for the Caribbean's largest population of red-footed boobies. The island also has the endangered green Cayman parrot. Over 40% of the land is wetlands, with mangrove-fringed lagoons and ponds, and there are bird viewing platforms with interpretative panels.

City of Atlantis statue
photo: Foots

Cayman Brac

Queen angelfish

After glitzy Grand Cayman, the pace of life changes dramatically once one gets to the laid-back island of Cayman Brac. Although small, the island has the most varied topography above land of the three Cayman isles. The normally calm northwest side is where the bulk of the diving is done.

The Brac has a fringing reef that surrounds the better part of the island. The north and south sides have different diving terrain, while the island's tips on the east and west get the most current and are the best bets for pelagic sightings. The west end also seems to get the most protection and has the bulk of dive sites, but with over 45 moored sites there is no shortage of places to dive.

Snorkeling is also very good, with lots of shallow inshore sites plus many large corals heads that come to within 10ft to 20ft of the surface. This, combined with superb water clarity, make a great spot for snorkelers and novice divers alike.

Dive boats and dive sites are primarily based on the south shore of the west end, so divers normally suit up once they get on board, as sites are close by. East end dives take a while longer and the Little Cayman Bloody Bay Marine

Park dives take about 45 minutes to get to on a good day.

On the north, the mini-wall starts at 20ft to 30ft, dropping to 50ft. The main wall then takes over and drops to 4,000ft, give or take a foot. Sponge life reigns here.

In the south, the spur and groove is the norm, running perpendicular to the shore it's easy to navigate but deeper, with the main wall at 60ft to 70ft. They don't quite have the sponge growth of the north, but the reef is pocked like a honeycomb with more tunnels, arches and swim-throughs.

Cayman Brac	GOOD SNORKELING	NOVICE	INTERMEDIATE	ADVANCED
52 AIRPORT REEF & WALL	•	•		
53 MV CAPTAIN KEITH TIBBETTS	•	•		
54 LOST CITY OF ATLANTIS	•	•		
55 CEMETERY WALL	•	•		
56 THE CHUTES	•	•		
57 SERGEANT MAJOR REEF	•	•		
58 WILDERNESS WALLL				•
59 ROCK MONSTER CHIMNEY				•

Upper deck of the Tibbets

52　AIRPORT REEF & WALL

Location: *North of West End Point, Cayman Brac*
Depth: *32-100ft (9-30m)*
Access: *Boat*
Range: *Novice to intermediate*

Off the island's west tip, obviously near the airport runway, are a couple of dives that offer the best of both worlds. Airport Reef is a shallow dive with a buoy in about 32ft of water, which divers and snorkelers can enjoy from depths of 15ft to about 50ft.

The shallow spur-and-groove system is punctuated by sea fans and sea plumes on the reeftop. There's good fish life here, including schools of grunts and angelfish. The site is also used for night dives and divers report seeing octopi roaming looking for shells and other prey. Reef crabs can also be found at night.

The wall dive buoy sits in deeper water. The dive starts at 65ft, marked by beautiful yellow and orange tube sponges, and steeply slopes down to 100ft, before dropping into the abyss.

The wall has some deep, large crevices with very nice marine growth, including rope sponges. Look for schools of big-eye jacks down deep and also grunts up at the 60ft level. It is not unusual to see gray angelfish and French angelfish. Coneys and groupers also seem to like this reef. Be careful, as one can have a tendency to go deep off the deep wall here.

Nearby, a site has been identified as an older wreck where ship ballast has been found. Locals think it could be the wreck of a pirate ship.

53 | **MV CAPTAIN KEITH TIBBETTS**

Location: *West of White Bay, Cayman Brac*
Depth: *40-90ft (13-27m)*
Access: *Boat*
Range: *All levels*

This wreck is one of the main attractions of The Sisters. It is where famous underwater explorer Jean Michel Cousteau literally went down with the ship. Sunk intentionally in 1996, the 300ft-long Brigadier Type Class II Frigate sits at a strong list to port in-between 50ft and 100ft of water.

The wreck's original name was *Patrol Vessel 356* and it was part of a Russian support group stationed in the Caribbean until the early 1990s. Before it was sunk, it was renamed MV *Captain Keith Tibbetts* in honor of a local Cayman pioneer seaman. The ship was made diver-safe by removing wires and doors before being flooded with water. Cousteau videotaped the sinking of the ship from his perspective in the bridge and now shows it to astonished dive groups when he lectures around the world.

Marine life now grows on the ship, which sits in a sandy basin and has attracted fish life as well. Three buoys are on the ship. The ship is cracked in the middle and the gun section at the stern is the place most divers, especially photographers, first visit. The stern guns are only slightly encrusted and very distinguishable. They make for great props and can be photographed with a diver model or stand-alone. Start deep and work your way up.

Shifting sands have covered a good portion of the wreck. The bridge is open and penetrable, but due to the wreck's breaking up some of the metal is sharp and jagged, so dive around it cautiously. Fish life includes great barracuda, queen angels and yellow tang. If you get tired of the wreck, there is also a nice reef about 50ft off starboard (the right side). Look also for garden eels in the sand around the ship.

Not too far from this ship is another wreck, the tugboat *Kissimmee*. It is somewhat shallower and can be dived by wreck buffs as a second dive. The *Cayman Mariner* in East Chute is also a similarly good wreck dive that's close by, but it is deeper and probably not suitable for a second dive as bottom time would be short.

Guns on the Tibbets

Juvenile queen angel in transition to adulthood

54 LOST CITY OF ATLANTIS

Location: *North of White Bay, Cayman Brac*
Depth: *30-50ft (9-16m)*
Access: *Boat*
Range: *All levels*

One of the greatest mythological cities in history, the lost city of Atlantis is now the newest dive site in the Cayman Islands. Just off Cayman Brac, a local artist is creating a new dive at Brac Reef Beach Resort by assembling the city first spoken of by Plato in 40ft to 50ft of water. It will eventually have more than 100 pieces of original sculpture cast from molds by local artist Foots. Using a blend of materials, crushed rock, sand and cement, ancient mythology meets in this vision of the ruins of Atlantis.

Phase one consists of the Archway of Atlantis and the Elders' Way, which is a pathway lined with eleven 5ft temple columns leading to the Inner Circle of Light, which is an enormous sundial and base weighing nearly 10,000lbs. And there's also the 18ft-tall Pyramid of Atlantis that weighs in excess of 40,000lbs.

Encrusting marine life has already taken to the structure, which is hoped to be a magnet for fish that will continually add to the look and mystique of the place. It is certainly a great prop for wide angle photography, and is good for macro as well with cleaning stations already established. Cleaner shrimp bring other forms of life to the site, and stingrays and eagle rays are in the area

The dive sits off the north shore of Cayman Brac in a large sandy area at a dive site called Radar Reef. This is home to parrotfish, lots of friendly yellowtail snappers and some angels. Nearby is a nice spur-and-groove reef which has some nice fans and sea plumes.

55 CEMETERY WALL

Location: *Cotton Tree Bay, Cayman Brac*
Depth: *50-130ft (15-130m)*
Access: *Shore & boat*
Range: *All levels*

This is one of the island's more beautiful walls with a good selection of hard corals and marine life. The dive starts in about 45ft where the upper reef crest is adorned in corals, such as healthy star and brain corals, then heads down a deep canyon that is adorned with thick and healthy plate coral, sponges and even black coral trees.

The main wall drop starts at around 65ft and falls into the abyss. The habitat here is good for all manner of smaller marine life. Look for cleaning stations with banded cleaner shrimp and wrasse, fairy basslets hovering just off the corals and even a few morays all in the protection of the rich coral growth. The sandy bottom is a favorite spot for southern stingrays which may be rooting about in the sand.

Along the wall look for large deepwater gorgonians, beautiful basket sponges and long tube sponges. Turtles and eagle rays are seen here on a regular basis. Occasionally look out into the blue, as Caribbean reef sharks have also been reported.

Divemasters sometimes bring divers up through a tunnel that starts at 90ft and comes back up to the upper wall.

Rope sponges along The Great Wall photo: J. Dietz

A saddled blenny poses for a photo

56   THE CHUTES

Location: *North of Airport, Cayman Brac*
Depth: *55-130ft (17-40m)*
Access: *Boat*
Range: *All levels*

There are three chute dives at Cayman Brac: west, middle and east chutes. All have similar profiles and hold nice marine life and some unusual surprises. The upper part of the reef is sandy with roaming stingrays that may be accom-panied by opportunistic bar jacks who may try to grab a morsel of food the rays may scare up. Each basin leads to a sand chute that is flanked by high coral spurs.

In some areas, jawfish have their holes and may be seen incubating eggs in their jaws. Dive down the chute, checking the sides of the spurs for hard corals which often hide arrowcrabs and also vase sponges. The chute eventually spills out to the wall and down to the depths.

Dive along the wall and look for the huge barrel sponges that sometimes serve as cleaning stations. Big tube sponges have small blennies that scurry

57 | SERGEANT MAJOR REEF

Location: *South of Channel Bay, Cayman Brac*
Depth: *32-50ft (10-15m)*
Access: *Boat*
Range: *Novice*

This dive can be done at many levels by day or by night. Sergeant Major Reef and nearby Butterfly Reef have a beautiful spur-and-groove system that starts in just 30ft and has lots going on. As most dives here are Point A to Point A, divers can wander over the reeftop looking for schoolmasters in the sea fans and healthy stands of golden elkhorn coral, trumpetfish lurking behind sea plumes and groupers waiting for a meal to swim by. Butterflyfish and parrotfish are also common here.

Deeper are growths of staghorns with their damsels. The site runs deeper down the grooves and there are some fun swim-throughs to be found, small tunnels and windows, and interesting reef formations.

Moray eels and spiny lobsters can be found in the cracks and crevices as this structure gives them good habitat and protection. The bigger ledges and overhangs also attract nurse sharks. Sea turtles, commonly hawksbills, like to sleep on the ledges if not foraging for hydroids.

All over the reef, look for cleaning stations that attract blue tangs, triggerfish, butterflyfish and groupers. Little spiny puffers also come here, and the white sand fingers also attract eagle rays and southern stingrays. Keep an eye out into the grooves for these beautiful rays. This is a very nice reef that can be dived many times without getting old. And at night, don't be surprised if you run into a big tarpon or three – they may follow you to see what your lights turn up.

about their surfaces. The reef crests at and below 100ft here, so your time exploring this luxuriant area may be short.

East chute probably holds the most interest of the three, as it seems to attract a greater variety of marine life. A shipwreck here, the *Cayman Mariner*, is a natural magnet for fish. At around 90ft is an old Spanish anchor that is embedded in the coral. It can be hard to see so ask your guide to point out this bit of Cayman history.

Make your way back up the wall and look around the reeftop for schoolmasters hovering near the fans and other such natural cover.

Bluestriped grunt

58 WILDERNESS WALL

Location: *South of Beach Point, Cayman Brac*
Depth: *46-100ft (14-30m)*
Access: *Boat*
Range: *Intermediate*

Snowy, white sand shallows starts in only 45ft of water here and are home to rays and peacock flounders. Follow any of these chutes and you will find tunnels and passages that head out the slope to the wall at 80ft to 100ft before dropping into the abyss.

The big attraction here is a pinnacle just off the wall at 100ft that is a current creator. This brings in big groupers, schooling horse-eye and yellow jacks and bug snappers. Eagle rays also come around this promontory.

The deep formations also create sponge-covered arches and all sorts of fascinating features. Look for azure vase sponges growing to nice sizes. Fish life includes Nassau grouper, which aren't overly common in the Caymans, angelfish and snapper. Also keep an eye out for scavenging sea turtles.

59 ROCK MONSTER CHIMNEY

Location: *South of Pollard's Bay, Cayman Brac*
Depth: *55-100ft (17-30m)*
Access: *Boat*
Range: *Intermediate to advanced*

Rock Monster Chimney is off one of the Brac's scenic bluff spots at Pollard's Bay. The bluff, rising 160ft, is a beautiful scenic backdrop for a dive. Below the sea, the reef is alive and the terrain unusual. The site is on the island's windward side and isn't always accessible, but it is worth a try when conditions are good.

Diamond blenny

Patch reefs, which hold several shrimp species and can be good for macro photography, cover the top of the site which starts at 50ft to 60ft. The sandy patches between the reef are haunts of southern stingrays.

The dive has a vertical swim-through coral chimney just east of the mooring. This feature can dwarf the diver and is well worth the swim.

On the deep and very sheer outer wall at Rock Monster Chimney, look for queen angelfish as well as large trumpetfish. Beautiful soft corals and big sponges highlight this depth change, while large scalloped plate corals create overhangs for lurkers. Enjoy this foray into the abyss and then head back up to the mooring.

A photographer approaches rope sponges

A hovering fairly basslet

Little Cayman Island

A young hawksbill sea turtle

The walls on this island are among the finest in the world, which is why divers endure the boat ride from Cayman Brac. Those who like wall diving are in heaven at most of this island's sites. The awe-inspiring walls can start as shallow at 20ft and fall vertically into oblivion.

Concern about overuse of the best wall sites, due to their popularity, has seen the marine park authority establish weekly dive quotas for dive shops visiting here. Only about 14 dives per Brac and Little Cayman shop are allowed per week, and live aboards also have similar limitations.

With over 50 dive sites and a tiny population base, you'll be able to do some – if not all – of the dives you want during the course of a week.

If the marina is blown-out by weather, the south side of the island also offers dives similar to those of Brac, with walls starting at around 50ft to 80ft.

Little Cayman Island's marine park designation has meant the fish and invertebrate life is quite plentiful and approachable. The island's reefs are known for stunning rope, barrel and tube sponge formations and healthy hard corals.

Little Cayman Island		GOOD SNORKELING	NOVICE	INTERMEDIATE	ADVANCED
60	EAGLE RAY ROUNDUP				•
61	CUMBER'S CAVES	•	•		
62	MIXING BOWL (THREE FATHOM WALL)	•	•		
63	MARILYN'S CUT	•	•		
64	RANDY'S GAZEBO (CHIMNEY)	•		•	
65	GREAT WALL EAST/WEST	•		•	
66	BARRACUDA BIGHT			•	
67	PATTY'S PLACE			•	
68	WINDSOCK REEF	•	•		

60 | EAGLE RAY ROUNDUP

Location: *West of Jackson's Bay, Little Cayman*
Depth: *29-100ft*
Access: *Boat*
Range: *Intermediate*

Located in Jackson's Bay, this site is known for its deepwater sea fans, lacey gorgonians and vase sponges, and frequent eagle ray and southern stingray sightings. The sandy upper reef, starting in only 29ft of water by the mooring, is a hunting area for the rays.

The wall here starts in just 40ft and drops off with sand chutes trailing down.

The wall isn't sheer and there are lots of places to explore. Divers can stay between 60ft and 80ft and see a lot. Tube sponges come in hues of purple and yellow, while blue chromis give life and color to the wall. Big bluehead parrotfish, jacks and yellowtail snapper are all here. The sand holds a good community of jawfish – look at each to see if any are incubating eggs. The sand is also home to a good-sized garden eel colony.

Spotted eagle rays circling

Poke around the wall for a while and then head back up shallow to see if any eagle rays are doing their thing in the sandy upper shelf.

61 | CUMBER'S CAVES

Location: *West of Jackson Bay, Little Cayman*
Depth: *13-130ft (4-40m)*
Access: *Shore & boat*
Range: *All levels*

Everyone from snorkelers, novices, advanced and even experienced deep divers can enjoy this dive – night dives are also very good at this site. Most divers arrive here by boat, but this site is also a good shore dive if you happen to have transport.

The reason Cumber's Caves is so much fun is that there are a number of cuts, crevices, coral arches and swim-throughs, providing lots of habitat and making the reef a real maze for divers to explore. Many tunnels and passages pop right out on the outer wall.

Fin out over the 45ft-deep sand plain and stingrays. One favorite spot is at the 45ft reef crest, where a cut has an old anchor wedged into the sand. A cave here allows the diver to descend through the sponge encrusted shaft from 40ft to an exit at 85ft. Look for shrimps and corals along the walls and perhaps a resting nurse shark. Be careful not to kick and stir up sand.

Experienced divers will like this wall section, with its beautiful rope sponges and big basket sponges. Head back up to the shallows and check the sand for jawfish, garden eels, conch and some anemones.

For shore divers, it's a healthy swim out to the mooring and an equally healthy swim and walk back in, so keep enough air to do it comfortably.

Deco stop on the clear wall waters

Schoolmasters and bluestriped grunts hover at a purple sea fan

A friendly snapper gets a kiss from a divemaster

| 62 | **MIXING BOWL (THREE FATHOM WALL)** |

Location: *The Jackson Bay & Bloody Bay Border, Little Cayman*
Depth: *18-130ft (5-40m)*
Access: *Boat*
Range: *All (deep-intermediate)*

This site is pretty much where Jackson's Bay stops and Bloody Bay and its famous wall starts. The Jackson's Bay area dog-legs out to a sandy channel 18ft-deep that parallels the shore. Snorkelers and those wanting a shallow dive will enjoy this area. The site's secondary moniker, 'Three Fathom Wall,' is due to the wall top being at 18ft (three fathoms).

Photographers will want to make a couple of dives here to take advantage of the very good macro life and excellent wide angle possibilities. Most dives descend the sand corridor down the Bloody Bay side to see the steep drop-off area and its marine life. A sandy slope running through the area can be followed to 100ft. The wall here is brilliant in a mind-boggling kaleidoscope of colors and shapes.

Sponge colors seem to run the gamut from reds to yellows, oranges and even white. Great habitat is everywhere, as the wall is cut and gouged with all kinds of overhangs, holes, swim-throughs and arches. Big yellowfin grouper, Nassau grouper and coneys all gather here, while the sponges also attract very good macro life. Keep an eye out for longlure frogfish and even seahorses.

Head back up the wall to the reeftop, where the hard corals and sea fans give shelter to schoolmasters, striped snappers and grunts. Look also for the large pillar coral stand that is often surrounded by flitting blue chromis.

A deco stop can be done in the sand above, where macro shooters can look for yellowhead jawfish and also southern stingrays.

Photogenic Nassau grouper
photo: J. Dietz

63	**MARILYN'S CUT**

Location: *Bloody Bay, Little Cayman*
Depth: *35-100ft (10-30m)*
Access: *Boat*
Range: *All levels*

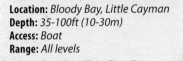

Sometimes called Hole in the Wall, Marilyn's Cut is a good dive to follow the guide on as it can have some currents and the wall does some strange things. But the amazing sponges here, combined with the chance to see pelagic fish, make this deep little dive worth it. This is a good wide angle dive for photographers.

Descend into a steep canyon off the wall from 30ft. Soon a range of sponges will come into view, including brilliant rope, yellow tube, rose-colored barrel, trumpet and cup sponges. Look for trumpetfish, scrawled filefish and groupers hanging out in the confines of this colorful maze.

The hole in the wall is to the right of a large coral mound and is really a large tunnel that runs parallel to the wall. It's a fun exploration – just keep track of your bottom time.

This site has a very friendly and photogenic grouper that has taken to divers – one can even pet it.

64	**RANDY'S GAZEBO (CHIMNEY)**

Location: *Bloody Bay, Little Cayman*
Depth: *30-100ft (9-30m)*
Access: *Boat*
Range: *Intermediate*

Yee-haw. Step off the top of this wall and descend into the abyss. Known for its vertical face, this dive site is full of massive barrel sponges with cleaning stations full of shrimp and yellowhead wrasse. Yellow tip anemones thrive in the environment, while schooling fish course along the wall and others hide in the confines of the drop-off. This is a sponge dive more than a big-time fish dive – big barrel sponges are the norm.

Start the dive by descending into a chimney at 40ft which opens out to the sheer wall at 75ft. Once on the wall, look at what the fish are doing. If there's a strong current, they'll be facing into it. If they are just milling around, the current is pretty slack. The current can also pick up where the wall forms some points and vertical canyons. The wall also leads to a natural coral arch, which divers often use as a frame to pose in front of.

The upper reef can have spotted rums, black durgon in the water column, butterflyfish and green sea turtles.

Rope sponges along the sheer wall

A diver looks at some sea plumes

65 | GREAT WALL EAST/WEST

Location: *North of Salt Pier, SW Coast, Cayman Islands*
Depth: *35-100ft (10-30m)*
Access: *Boat*
Range: *Intermediate*

At the west end of Bloody Bay Marine Park, this is one of the main diving attractions in the Caymans and the Caribbean. The drop-off here is at 90 degrees and the heavily overgrown wall is undercut in some areas. Although you can go as deep as Davey Jones' locker here, the wall is so rich that depth isn't really necessary.

Diving can be done in the 50ft to 90ft range and you'll see black coral trees, huge plating coral formations, barrel sponges and stunning tube sponge growths. Look for black durgon, groupers, eagle rays out in the blue, and many types of jacks – including horse-eyes and yellow jacks. Sea turtles and even Caribbean reef sharks have been seen with some regularity here.

The reetop at 35ft to 40ft is also nice, so even novice divers can experience the sight. Look for brown sponges, coral clusters and trumpetfish. This is a premier dive site and wide angle photographer's dream.

66 | BARRACUDA BIGHT

Location: *Bloody Bay, Little Cayman*
Depth: *30-100ft (9-30m)*
Access: *Boat*
Range: *Intermediate*

At Bloody Bay Wall's western end, Barracuda Bight has nice outcrops of hard corals that extend off the wall and are covered in rope and vase sponges. Look for the mountainlike formations of star corals that attract clouds of blue chromis. They are quite the eye-popping sight.

At 30ft, take the swim-through out to the wall's edge, a rich area where anything can show up. Big moray eels live here and are often seen free-swimming as they look for food or roam from their dens. Big sea turtles also come into the wall to rest and munch on sponges.

The fish schools here are healthy and thick. Yellowtail snapper and blue-striped grunts are well-represented.

Christmas tree worm

Tube sponges get a nibble from a four-eye butterflyfish.

Divers descend to the reef

Location: *Preston Bay, Little Cayman*
Depth: *30-60ft*
Access: *Boat*
Range: *All levels*

Windsock Reef is made for underwater photographers. It is shallow enough for a nice long dive and has plenty of photo subjects – especially fish life, macro critters and invertebrates, such as shrimp and shells. The site can even surprise with something big like a sleeping nurse shark.

The airport's windsock is visible from here, hence the name. Underwater, the reef is a series of patch reefs with sponge growth, corals, soft corals and sandy patches in-between.

Fish life includes whitespotted filefish, southern stingrays, bigeyes, spiny puffers, coneys and soldierfish peering out from the corals. At night, the red fish like bigeyes and soldierfish can be seen away from the reef. Macro buffs will find the 105mm lens handy for all the goby life.

Look for an old cannon near the mooring.

67 PATTY'S PLACE

Location: *Preston Bay, Little Cayman*
Depth: *65-120ft (20-40m)*
Access: *Boat*
Range: *Intermediate*

Similar to The Brac or sites off Cobalt Coast on Grand Cayman, this site has some nice stands of elkhorn coral which attract a variety of schooling fish, including striped snapper, grunts and schoolmasters. But most divers head deeper to the deep spur-and-groove system. Follow the groove down deep to where it bottoms out at a cut at 120ft (near limit of sport diving). Get an eyeful of the plate corals and nice sponge life in this stunning cut, which make it worth a short trip, then make your way back up.

Up at 60ft there are nice tube sponge formations, some jawfish in the rubble bottom and flitting schools of chromis. Look around here until its time to move up the mooring and give yourself at least five minutes deco time to off-gas.

Stoplight parrotfish

Marauding surgeonfish come in close to feed

Marine Life

lettuce sea slug

The Caymans have a large fish population and an equally diverse invertebrate population, opening the door for the study of some very colorful and unique creatures. Fish, crabs and other marine creatures have specific habitats. Getting to know where a certain subject likes to live, when it likes to feed, when and where it mates and all of the other routines of life under the sea will enable the diver to find the subject with greater ease. This enhances observation, makes diving more interesting and also aids photography.

Colorful fish are perhaps the most sought in the Cayman Islands' waters. Beautiful angelfish, parrotfish, basslets and triggerfish all catch the eye of a diver or snorkeler. But there are more mundane fish that are also worth watching for their unique coloration or ability to camouflage, like a seahorse of frogfish.

The invertebrate world around the Cayman Islands can't be dismissed. The amazing sponge formations on virtually every dive site give the reef form and color. Cayman Island corals are healthy and very competitive. Crustaceans like shrimp, crabs and lobsters all have unique homes, and many have symbiotic relationships with other marine creatures.

Following is a small sampling of some of the Cayman Islands' undersea life.

HAZARDOUS MARINE LIFE

Many marine animals have developed chemical weapons to aid them in their struggle against each other, and these weapons are often effective against humans. Perhaps the most common venomous creature in Cayman waters is fire coral. These waters occasionally see jellyfish in the form of the Portuguese man-of-war, the long-spined black sea urchin and two worms – the fireworm and the red-tipped fireworm – are also capable of causing trouble. The stingrays and the two kinds of scorpionfishes are the only venomous fish of concern in this region. Cone shells are also highly venomous. Some common creatures, like eels and barracuda, can deliver a nasty bite, although it is quite rare. Seeing a shark is not all that common, much less getting bitten by one.

Divers should read or ask about which creatures will be commonly seen and should know first aid procedures in the rare event that a person is wounded by a marine animal. Be especially careful on night dives. Carrying proper antiseptic ointment greatly helps in the event of coral cuts and minor abrasions.

Barracuda

Fire Coral

Fire coral looks pretty, with its caramel color, but it is like putting your hand on a cigarette. It actually has tiny 'hairs' that burn like crazy and can swell up afterward. This mechanism is to defend against munching parrotfish, but divers sometimes get tagged as well. If stung by their powerful nematocysts, the skin will burn and itch. Rinse with seawater or water and apply vinegar or methylated alcohol on the sting. In a severe case try antihistamines and seek immediate medical treatment.

Barracuda

Barracuda bites are quite rare. The fish tend to be attracted to shiny objects and have been known to attack in murky water. Like sharks, this is normally a case of mistaken identity and invariably an accident.

On Cayman Island reefs, small schools and individual blackbar barracuda will frequently be encountered. There are also a lot of the larger great barracuda. These fish should not be teased. Their bites can be damaging, so stop any bleeding, reassure the patient, treat for shock and seek immediate medical treatment.

Bristleworms

While they may seem soft and fluffy, they can deliver a painful sting. Each of the bristleworm's body segments has a pair of small parapodia, or paddle-shaped appendages. These have embedded tiny hairs or bristle-like pieces. Bristleworms have well-developed sense organs with a kind of head with eyes, antennae and sensory palps. Pick out the hairs using tweezers or duct tape and submerge the sting in very hot water for 30 to 60 minutes. If the victim has a history of venom allergies, seek immediate medical treatment.

Jellyfish

The stings of a jellyfish are released by nematocysts contained in the trailing tentacles. Nematocysts are the tiny stinging cells found in jellyfish, anemones and corals which are used both for defense and for capturing live food. They are triggered by a variety of stimuli, including contact with human skin. When fired a tiny spring-loaded dart is fired into the organism and venom is injected. Once fired, they can never be reloaded and a new one must replace it.

The rule of thumb is the longer the tentacles, the more painful the sting. On the outer reefs, Portuguese Man-o-war are seasonally found. Larval jellies sometimes appear and can get into the wetsuit, which is a real pain. Most stings can be treated with vinegar. Some people do react adversely to jellyfish stings, similar to those who are allergic to bee stings. Be prepared to administer CPR and seek medical aid.

Bristleworm

Sea Urchins

In 1983, the long-spined black sea urchin suffered a Caribbean-wide mass mortality as a result of a waterborne pathogen. Numbers fell so low that the population is only now beginning to recover. These creatures form an important function on reefs by feeding on algae which might otherwise overgrow the slow growing corals. Their disappearance meant that many reefs were overgrown and killed by algae. The stings from the spines can range from irritating to highly intense. Spines can also break off inside the skin. Avoid contact with urchins and remain vigilant in the areas they frequent, especially at night. Treat urchin spines with a citric acid like lemon or lime juice to break down the spine. Treat by administering CPR until the pain subsides. Seek medical advice and use antibiotics where advised. Spines may have to be surgically removed.

Caribbean reef shark
photo: J. Dietz

Sharks

Sharks are encountered on few dives in Cayman Islands. Attacks are rare and usually only occur in some misguided feeding attempt or to fishermen spearing fish. In the event a shark does become aggressive, it is sometimes wise to rise to a shallower depth to get out of its territory. If it comes too close, stop and face the animal and watch it closely and quietly. Be prepared to push it away with a camera, knife, spear or tank. Treatment for bites is to stop any bleeding, reassure the patient and treat for shock, and seek immediate medical treatment.

Stingrays

Stingrays have one or more four- to eight-inch serrated venomous sheathed barbs that are sharp and can be used to ward off enemies. These can inflict a painful wound in humans that can quickly infect. If the barb breaks off, it must be surgically removed. Do not try to pull it out. Reports of stings and accidents at popular Cayman sites like **Stingray City** and **Sandbar** are actually very rare. The wound can also be quite painful with a lot of swelling. To treat, wash the wound, immerse in water as hot as the victim can stand for 60 to 90 minutes to break down venom, and seek immediate medical aid.

Stonefish/Scorpionfish

These fish will be seen commonly in sandy and rubbly areas in Cayman Island waters and on night dives. They inject their venom through the spines on their back. The wound can also be quite painful with a lot of swelling. To treat, wash the wound, immerse in water as hot as the victim can stand for 60 to 90 minutes and seek medical aid.

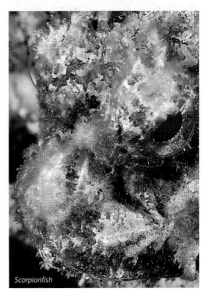
Scorpionfish

A stingray sculpture highlights the downtown area

Travel Facts

Tour ship daytrippers fill the George Town streets

GETTING THERE

Many international airlines have daily services to the Cayman Islands, which are located in the Western Caribbean, 480 miles south of Miami, Florida; 150 miles south of Cuba; and 180 miles northwest of Jamaica. By air, the Cayman Islands are only a 70-minute flight from Miami.

Most international passengers arrive at Owen Roberts International Airport a couple miles from George Town on Grand Cayman. Some flights also serve Cayman Brac's Gerrard Smith International Airport. The best access to the islands is from the US, and numerous carriers have regular flights between Grand Cayman and Florida's Miami, Fort Lauderdale, Tampa and Orlando. Airlines also offer direct services from Houston, Atlanta, Memphis, Pittsburgh, Indianapolis, Chicago, Boston, Newark and other US cities. Cayman Airways has a few flights between US cities and Cayman Brac. Air Canada flies direct from Toronto, and British Airways flies direct from London-Heathrow. There are also flights between George Town and Jamaica on Air Jamaica.

Cruise ships regularly dock at George Town on Grand Cayman and at Creek on Cayman Brac.

GETTING AROUND

Cayman Airways has daily flights to the Sisters islands.

Grand Cayman Island has well-maintained roads and highways that allow divers to explore the entire island. Rental cars are recommended and your hotel can usually arrange for a week-long package with your hotel accommodation. Do reserve a car in advance as they are in demand. You have to be at least 21 years old to rent a car.

Traffic flow is to the left side of the road, as in Great Britain (Americans take note!). Local driving standards, the risk of accidents, the availability of emergency roadside service, quality and frequency of signage, and enforcement of traffic laws, generally meet or exceed the standards of the United States. Visitors must obtain a temporary driver's license, easily granted upon presentation of a valid state driver's license and payment of a small fee, at a car rental agency or police station.

Be aware that laws against driving while intoxicated are strictly enforced. Don't drink and drive. Take a taxi instead. Seatbelt laws are also enforced and require the driver and all passengers to be fastened in while in motion.

From bikes to buses there are many ways to get around

If you are diving through your hotel dive shop, they will provide transportation between the hotel and boat dock and back again. If you like to hang around the hotel, no car is needed.

Traffic and parking in downtown George Town can be very bad – especially when the cruise ships are depositing people. The beach road changes names frequently, but is the same strip of asphalt and runs along the beach and shoreline as South Church Street, Harbour Drive, North Church Street, West Bay Road and Northwest Point Road. There is a new central road that bypasses much of the Seven Mile Beach strip road and also connects to many through streets that run off the beach road. Take this highway to get to the East End access and central shopping areas quickly.

Taxis are available at Owen Roberts International Airport on Grand Cayman and offer a fixed rate per vehicle or per person to all points on Grand Cayman. Information is available from the taxi dispatcher at the curb. Oddly, hotel vans can not and do not provide courtesy arrival pickup at the airport. Taxis are also available from all resorts and from the taxi stand at the cruise ship dock in George Town. A sign with current rates is posted at the dock.

There are several private limousine services on Grand Cayman, for special events and airport transfers.

Grand Cayman also has a public bus transportation system. The new bus terminal is located adjacent the Public Library on Edward St in downtown George Town and serves as the dispatch point for buses to all districts. There are 38 mini-buses operated by 24 licensed operators, serving eight routes. Daily service starts at 6am and runs to between 9pm and 11pm depending on the route.

Many local people also ride bikes, particularly on the Sisters islands.

If you really want to have fun, take a scheduled charter or charter your own Cayman Islands helicopter flight. It will soar over **Stingray City** and the blue waters of North Sound and fly over the West Bay so you can see the spurs and grooves you dive daily. Bring your polaroids and put the polarizer on your camera lens.

ENTRY REQUIREMENTS

Citizens of the US, Canada, EU, the UK or the Commonwealth, Israel and Japan do not require visas. Travelers from elsewhere may need visas prior to entry. Contact the nearest British Consulate, Embassy or High Commission to obtain visa applications.

The Cayman Islands aims to ensure that visitors are able to proceed through customs and immigration in an efficient and hassle-free manner. Visitors that deplane in Grand Cayman are welcomed by the sweet sound of live music as they proceed into the arrivals lounge. Professional immigration and custom service agents process visitor documentation and get you on your way to enjoy your vacation. Even upon leaving, personal baggage inspection is done randomly and courteously. It is a refreshing and civil way to ensure security while maintaining the peace of mind that visitors no doubt head home with after a week of Cayman relaxation.

All US citizens traveling by air between the United States and the Caribbean, Canada, Mexico, Central and South American and Bermuda are required to present a valid passport. Keep the immigration card that is given to you upon arrival as you must present this when departing.

For further information on entry into the Cayman Islands, contact the Cayman Islands Department of Immigration (☎ (345) 949-8052).

There is a CI$20.00 or US$25.00 departure tax for the Cayman Islands that is almost always included in the price of your airline ticket.

TIME

The Cayman Islands are on Atlantic Standard Time that is the same as the US east coast during Daylight Saving Time (mid-Spring to mid-Fall).

The Cayman Islands does not change time for Daylight Saving. When it's noon in Cayman Islands it is 3pm (next day) in Sydney, Australia; 9pm in San Francisco, California; and 5am in London, England.

MONEY

The Cayman dollar, first issued in 1972, is the official currency and is sometimes referred to as the CD. It has a basic dollar unit, issued in notes with denominations of CI$1, CI$5, CI$10, CI$25, CI$50 and CI$100, and coins valued at 1, 5, 10 and 25 cent/s. The CI dollar has a fixed exchange rate with the US dollar of CI$1 to US$1.25. Or, the US dollar equals CI$.80.

A shoreside restaurant along the rugged northeast coast

A sailboat cruises the northern reefs

There is no need for visitors to exchange their US dollars into local currency. There are so many American tourists that the dollar is widely accepted, but expect your change to be in Cayman bills and coins.

Canadian dollars, Euro dollars and pounds sterling can be exchanged for CI dollars at local banks, which are open 10am to 3pm Monday to Friday. ATMs accepting VISA and MasterCard with Cirrus affiliation are located at Cayman National Bank and other banks, at Owen Roberts International Airport, all over the touristy part of Georgetown, and a few other locations, such as the grocery stores.

All of the major credits cards (with the exception of the Discover Card) and travelers checks are widely accepted at hotels, restaurants, taverns and auto rental agencies. Be sure to have your passport or positive ID when changing traveler's checks at banks (which, by the way, do not give a better rate of exchange!).

ELECTRICITY

All electricity in the Cayman Islands is 110V, 60Hz. A two-pronged wall socket similar to the US plug is used. Some sockets do not have a third ground hole so it is advisable to bring an adapter to make your cord plug two-pronged. Many chargers, like the Ikelite super charger, come equipped to handle 100/240 volts and are fine. Most laptop computer power sources, like the Mac iBook, also have these. These are the handiest way to get your equipment charged up and staying that way.

Most US appliances, like your electric toothbrush, will work. Some of the dive shops and resorts have stations for guest use for charging camera batteries and strobes. This may be a viable way to prevent problems with charging.

The Cayman Islands does occasionally have surges and brownouts. If you plug anything electronically delicate into a wall outlet, consider bringing a small surge protector to place in-between.

Shell & Black Coral Products

The taking of shells and other natural artifacts is strictly prohibited in the Cayman Islands. Still, items using shells and marine creatures can be found. These are normally shipped in from places like Indonesia and the Philippines and can often be seen in the form of products like bracelets and earrings. Please discourage the creation of these products by not purchasing such items and letting store-owners know that you disapprove of seeing these items on the shelves.

There are also some amazing black coral sculptures available at galleries. The galleries that sell these items are often vague about where the black coral actually comes from. Demand a firm answer or maybe just walk away from these items as well.

If you are offered a wildlife product or natural item for sale, ask questions about the product's origin. If the vendor seems poorly informed, think twice about your actions. Otherwise, your purchase could encourage continued illegal trade in wildlife and be confiscated either before you leave the Cayman Islands or on your return home.

When in doubt, don't buy and don't take. Leave it in the sea or at the store. Officials are quick to point out that anyone violating Cayman Island's marine environment ordinance is subject to prosecution and heavy fines.

WEIGHTS & MEASURES

The Imperial system of weights and measures is used. Depths are usually registered in feet and weights in pounds. All sale and rental dive gear is oriented this way. See our quick conversion scale on the back inside cover.

TELECOMMUNICATIONS

Email outlets and Internet cafes are becoming increasingly prevalent all over the Caymans. Many hotels have computes centers, business centers and wireless weeklong packages. Some have free wireless in their café areas and even throughout the hotel. Email and Internet providers normally feature fast DSL Internet. Some public places offer wireless hotspots which you can tap into by buying a local network card.

Calls from Cayman Islands to the US are easily made through your hotel switchboard or direct dial from your room. To tell your jealous friends how good the diving is, a phone call can also be made from public phones using a Cable & Wireless prepaid phone card. You can also use a credit card (☎ 1-800-CALL-USA) but it costs a bundle.

You can rent a phone for the week at the Cable & Wireless retail store in George Town. Cell phones compatible with 800Mhz or TMDA networks can roam in the islands.

The Cayman country code is 345.

Accommodation runs from scenic inns like this to 5-star hotels

ACCOMMODATION

There are hotels for every budget and desire, but since most divers have equipment and often-pricey photo gear, it is best to seek out the more up-scale hotels to avoid problems. Since this island is not a cheap place to stay, that's pretty easy to do. The best deals come in the form of dive packages that provide reasonable weekly room rates or condominiums. Backpacker hostels are also available.

The dive hotels closest to the night-life are right on the western shoreline at the famous Seven Mile Beach. There are also many other options, including seaside hotels like Boatswain's Bay's Cobalt Coast or East End's Compass Point, which have their own charm set away from the main drag. Guesthouses, time-shares, villas, condos and even personal homes can be rented by those staying for a while or wanting extra comforts. Dining out isn't cheap in the Caymans, so renting a place with self-catering facilities can be economical. The stores are well-stocked.

Cayman Brac also has a diverse selection of resorts, hotels and condominiums. The quieter Little Cayman isn't quite as built up but has options for visitors seeking a relaxing getaway or an adventurous dive vacation.

POSTAL

Mail leaves the islands regularly and gets delivered in a reasonable amount of time. For post cards, the local post office is just fine – you can even post a postcard from Hell, with a Hell post-mark. Air Parcel Post may be the most reasonable, but not fastest, way to send things. Express Mail Service (EMS) provides a fast (though not overnight), efficient, reliable and fully documented service to over 140 countries.

Local mail posted on Grand Cayman by 10am Monday to Friday will be delivered to any Grand Cayman postal destination the next day. Mail posted in Cayman Brac and Little Cayman by 10am Monday to Friday will be delivered to any Cayman Islands postal destination within three days. But this may be influenced by factors affecting air travel.

Rely on FedEx or DHL if you are sending anything valuable or requiring timely delivery.

Celebrating Big Blue

The Blue Dragon Trail on Grand Cayman is an interesting outdoor art exhibit that features Komodo dragon-sized Grand Cayman blue iguanas. The Grand Cayman blue iguana is the most endangered iguana in the world and artists from around the Caymans have taken to painting larger-than-life replicas of it to celebrate the lizard's struggle. The fun and colorful art pieces, 15 in all, are found in just about every corner of Grand Cayman.

Diners can watch divers enter the water from tableside while enjoying island cuisine

The Cayman Islands Department of Tourism ensures that hotels comply with all standards set out in the Tourism Accommodations Law, including ongoing inspections.

DINING & FOOD

The Cayman Islands are blessed with a great variety of restaurants that offer everything from fresh sushi to Jamaican jerk. Seafood is high on the menu of many eateries and since there is a turtle farm on the island, you may find turtle and conch on some menus and in small local restaurants like those along the north shore. Local foods include dishes like Cayman-style fish in spicy tomato and onion sauce, Jamaican beef patties, red-bean soup, jerk pork, conch chowder, conch fritters and rum cakes. There is also a local beer called, what else, Stingray Beer.

The restaurants of Grand Cayman are, on the whole, not cheap. But the food quality is generally excellent. The island does have a bunch of fast food joints but also has the fine cuisines of the world. Delis like Azzurro are top notch, Café de Sol has nice coffees, Ragazzi Ristorante is a real touch of class, and the Cobalt Coast and Rum Point Club offer nice food and a great sunset venue. Eats and Treats are both good options, with Treats having an adjacent and happening sports bar. The list is endless and you'd have to stay a month to sample every cuisine.

Self-caterers will find that the supermarkets, bakeries and liquor stores on Grand Cayman provide an extremely wide range of items. They usually have a good selection of cheeses, sliced meats, fresh baked goods and other munchies that you can stash in the room for between dive snacks. Wines come from all over the world.

cakes are also a b
come in more flavo
a Jimmy Buffet bar
CDs and have a 'rit

Many hotels have
goods and clothes from well-know
signers. Even if you've been diving all
week you can go home smelling like
Chanel. The 24K-Mon Art Gallery and
jewelry shop on Seven Mile Beach has
some innovative marine life sculptures.

Pretty much everything you want is
here (there's no Apple Store yet, however) if you look at the tourist and local
shopping centers. For a small place,
there's a lot going on and a lot to buy.

Divers will find a number of large and
extremely well-equipped dive supply
stores along West Bay Road.

ACTIVITIES & ATTRACTIONS

There are plenty of things to do in Cayman Islands besides diving. The islands
offer action and casual sports, including
road biking and mountain biking, hiking, rappelling at Cayman Brac, fishing
charters, historic tours, bird watching,
parasailing, water skiing, body board-
ing and many combinations of these
activities.

Celebrated on all three islands is Pirate's Week, a 10-day party at the end of
October that features fireworks, mock
battles and assorted skullduggery, and
gives bankers, bar workers and locals
the chance to break out the gold earrings, eye patches and stuffed parrots.

SHOPPING

The gift shops around George Town and
hotel dive shops have a colorful selection of goods ranging from the usual
Caribbean fare of Cayman pirate T-shirts
and some attractive local art, mostly in
the form of paintings and photography.
Island Glassblowing Studio is a great
little glass-blowing shop on the waterfront just north of the cruise ship terminal. Stephen and son Victor Zawistowski
turn out one-of-a-kind art pieces of
conchs, dolphins, rays and turtles that
make excellent Christmas ornaments.

There is a market open almost every
day across from the Port Authority that
caters to cruise ship visitors and offers
carvings, local crafts, clothes and T-shirts
and some great sea salt. The downtown
stores have beautiful porcelain products and all manner of Duty Free goods,
including the famed Tortuga rums. Rum

Kite surfing is gaining popularity in the Caymans

p Sub

This plunge along Cayman's famous wall into the abyss was on hold at the time of research due to the tourism hiatus following Hurricane Ivan. Enquire about deep sub dives close to your time of departure.

Grand Cayman's answer to Carnivale is Batabano, a weekend of costumed hedonism and hangovers held around Easter. The local equivalent on Cayman Brac is known as Brachanal, held a week after Batabano.

The hip little National Gallery of the Cayman Islands (Ground fl, waterfront, Harbor Place; www.nationalgallery.org.ky; open 9am-5pm Mon-Fri, 11am-4pm Sat), established in 1996, gives the Caymans' fledgling visual art scene room to breathe. Small, but creative in its use of space, the exhibits include electronic, audio and visual presentations in a relaxed atmosphere. Avant-garde displays make this little place worth a stop. There's always some local art on display and there's a tiny gift shop with some tasteful offerings. It is opposite the beachside Paradise Bar & Grill and snorkel site.

Also be sure to check out Pedro St. James Castle museum (www.pedro stjames.ky; open 9:30am-5pm daily). This imposing Caribbean great house dates from 1780, making it the oldest building in the Caymans, and it's been everything from a jail to a courthouse to parliament before recent refurbishments turned it into a museum. The Castle is touted as the islands' 'birthplace of democracy': in 1831 the decision was made here to vote for elected representatives. Just as momentously, this is the place where the Slavery Abolition Act was read in 1835. It now houses a museum featuring a multimedia presentation evoking 18th century Cayman, while the grounds showcase native flora.

WILDLIFE

Grand Cayman's botanic park is hard to beat and absolutely the best place to experience the island's indigenous fauna. A well-marked mile-long trail winds through lush, easy terrain, featuring about 300 native species. You'll see buttonwood swamps, mahogany forests and an excellent collection of native palms. The park is home to orchids (in bloom from late May through June) and the Floral Color Garden, which bursts with tropical flowers. You'll see turtles, lizards and parrots.

The Cayman blue iguana is an impressive lizard and a highly endangered species that's being studied at a captive breeding and reintroduction facility here (it's not open to the public, but you can occasionally see a couple of iguanas loitering near the entrance to the woodland trail). A full grown male can reach over 7ft from head to tail and move like the wind. Large older animals are a pale green to gray, while younger ones are a stunning lime blue. Some people think male iguanas have a sexual magic as they have two penises. They also know how to choose food with the highest nutrition and eat only fruits and greens. How did they reach the endangered point? Well, they are also a favorite ingredient in local stews.

Pods from the annatto tree

The rare wild blue iguana of the Caymans

North Sound and Sandbar

A diver greets French angelfish

The Sisters islands have five seabird colonies – red-footed booby, brown booby, magnificent frigate bird, white-tailed tropicbird and least tern. There are also 115 species of migrant land birds. These come mainly from North America, although some South and Central American migrants can also be found. Even flamingos have been seen. Over 70 species of non-breeding wetland migrants have also been observed.

On Grand Cayman, the mangroves hold many of the same birds and are a great place to see birdlife.

SAFETY

The Cayman Islands are considered politically stable and enjoy a high standard of living. The streets are also generally safe and even hotels report few incidents of break-ins or any such petty crime. It is one of the safer places to dive and visit anywhere in the world.

RECOMMENDED BOOKS

Reef Fish Identification: Florida Caribbean Bahamas by Paul Humann and Ned DeLoach (New World Publications).

Reef Coral Identification and Reef Creature Identification by Paul Humann and Ned DeLoach (New World Publications). *Hurricane Book* by Courtney Platt.

My Underwater Photo Journey by Cathy Church.

TOURIST OFFICES

Cayman Islands
Tourism Corporation
PO Box 67
Grand Cayman KY1-1102
☎ (345) 949-0623
www.caymanislands.ky

United States
☎ 1-877-4 CAYMAN

Canada
234 Eglinton Avenue East, Suite 306
Toronto, ON Canada M4P 1K5
☎ (416) 485-1550 or (800) 263-5808

UK
Arlington Street
London SW1A 1RE, United Kingdom
☎ +44 (0) 20 7491 7771
www.caymanislands.co.uk

A snorkeler observes a sea star in
the grasses of the North Sound

Listings

Net floats along the East Side

SELECTING A DIVE OPERATOR

Question everything when looking for the dive operation with which you're going to spend your hard-earned holiday time and money. Get satisfactory answers about the operation you are planning to dive with, the type of equipment, boat and its maintenance, divemasters, insurance coverage, cost of diving, the knowledge of the travel agent you are booking with. Check the Internet, and send plenty of emails.

There are many reputable operators in the Cayman Islands. The dive operators have a close-knit and pro-active association, the Cayman Islands Tourism Association (CITA). It has high safety standards and members must comply with the rules and regulations of this association. These regulations insure reasonable equipment, staff training and guest ratios, and the association ensures that guests are looked after well. Make sure your dive shop or tour boat belongs to it. It will insure the shop is adhering to certain high standards the association created for itself. For your own safety, peace of mind, value for money and quality of holiday, it pays to be a wise consumer in the Cayman Islands and anywhere else in the diving world.

Catching some rays in the Caymans!

GRAND CAYMAN

Cayman Aggressor IV
PO Box 1440, Morgan City, LA 70381
Toll Free:800-348-2628
☎ 985-385-2628
www.aggressor.com

Cayman Diving School
PO Box 31064 SMB, Grand Cayman
☎ 345-949-4729
www.caymandivingschool.com

Divers Down
PO Box 1706 GT, Grand Cayman
☎ 345-945-1611
www.diversdown.net

Diver's Supply
PO Box 31013 SMB, Grand Cayman
☎ 345-949-7621
Email: diversup@candw.ky

DiveTech
PO Box 31435 SMB, Grand Cayman
☎ 345-946-5658
www.divetech.com

Eden Rock Diving Centre, Ltd.
PO Box 1907 GT, Grand Cayman
☎ 345-949-7243
www.edenrockdive.com

Indigo Divers
PO Box 30445 SMB, Grand Cayman
☎ 345-525-3932
www.indigodivers.com

Kirk Sea Tours
PO Box 30268, Grand Cayman
☎ 345-949-7278
www.kirkseatours.com

Neptune's Divers
PO Box 30520 SMB, Grand Cayman
☎ 345-945-3990
www.neptunesdivers.com

Ocean Frontiers
PO Box 200 EE, Grand Cayman
Toll Free:800-348-6096
☎ 345-947-7500 or 345-947-0000
www.oceanfrontiers.com

Off The Wall Divers
PO Box 30176 SMB, Grand Cayman
☎ 345-945-7525
www.otwdivers.com

Peter Milburn's Dive Cayman, Ltd.
PO Box 596, Grand Cayman
☎ 345-945-5770
www.petermilburndivecayman.com

Deep Blue Divers (formerly Red Baron Diving)
PO Box 11369 APO, Grand Cayman
☎ 345-949-9116
www.redbarondivers.com

Red Sail Sports
PO Box 31473 SMB, Grand Cayman
Toll Free: 877-RED-SAIL (877-733-7245)
☎ 345-945-5965
www.redsailcayman.com

Seasports
PO Box 431 WB, Grand Cayman
☎ 345-949-3965
www.bestdivingingrandcayman.com

Sunset Divers
PO Box 479 GT, Grand Cayman
Toll Free:800-854-4767
☎ 345-949-7111
www.sunsethouse.com

Wall to Wall Diving
PO Box 31412 SMB, Grand Cayman
☎ 345-945-6608
www.walltowalldiving.com

LITTLE CAYMAN

Conch Club Divers
PO Box 42, Little Cayman
Toll Free: 800-327-3835
☎ 345-948-1026
www.conchclub.com

Sam McCoy's Diving & Fishing Lodge
PO Box 12, Little Cayman
Toll Free:800-626-0496
☎ 345-948-0026
www.mccoyslodge.com.ky

Pirates Point Resort
PO Box 43 LC, Little Cayman
☎ 345-948-1010
piratespointresort.com

Reef Divers - Little Cayman Beach Resort
4127 5th Ave., St. Petersburg
Toll Free: 800-327-3835
☎ 345-948-1070
www.littlecayman.com

Southern Cross Club
PO Box 44 LC, Little Cayman
☎ 345-948-1099
www.southerncrossclub.com

CAYMAN BRAC

Reef Divers – Brac Reef Beach Resort
PO Box 56, West End, Cayman Brac
Toll Free:800-327-3835
☎ 345-948-1642
www.bracreef.com

Index

Notes